A GUIDE TO CREATING SIGILS

AND HOW TO

MAKE THEM WORK FOR YOU

BY

VINCENT K. LUCE

A Guide to Creating Sigils and How to make them Work for You

By Vincent K. Luce

All rights reserved. No part of this book may be reproduced in part or whole in any format whatsoever without first contacting the author for permission.

To contact the author, please refer to the publisher's website:

www.darkmoonpress.com

Or send an SASE to:

P.O. Box 11496, Fort Wayne, Indiana 46858-1496

A Guide to Creating Sigils and How to make them Work for You

ISBN-13: 978-1492948797

Disclaimer: The author and publishers of this book do not take responsibility for anything used within or actions taken by anyone as a result of reading it. The publisher and author expressly disclaim responsibility for any unforeseen consequences arising from the information contained herein. The information provided and the opinions stated within this book are not guaranteed to produce any particular results. The strategies and advice contained within this printed work may not be suitable for every individual. It is assumed that the reader is a responsible and reasonable individual. This book is considered for learning purposes only and may in fact be a complete work of fiction depending on what lens you view it with.

Table of Contents

Introduction 12
    Why do sigils work? 15
    To know, to dare, to will, to keep silent 16
    What you can do with this book 16

Begin 18

Words of warning 22

ROBERT ANTON WILSON 24

GIORDANO BRUNO 26

What is the Method Used? 28

Getting Started… 30
    Step One - Determining you goal 30
    Step Two - Working with your sentence of intention 33
    Step Three - Boiling down your sentence of intent 36
    Step Four - Charging the sigil 38
    Specific Examples of Charging 39

A Second Method of Sigil Creation 42
    Base for sigil 44

Anagram to Symbol Method 46

Meanings behind the symbols within The Knight, Death and the Devil 48

THE KNIGHT, DEATH AND THE DEVIL 48

A breakdown of a hypersigil 49

Eliphas Levi's Sabbatical Goat 56

Sigil of Baphomet 56

    Breakdown of Sigil Elements 56

Creating a sigil/Charging Box 58

    Unfolded Sigil Box 62

    What to do with unused, old, no longer needed sigils 64

Creating the Chapel of the Infinite Reader (CHIR) 66

An Example of a Hypersigil Creation 66

The Sigils and their Creation 70

    Charging Symbol 1: 70

    Symbol 2: J. Krishnamurti 71

    Charging symbol 2 72

    Charging Symbol 3 73

    Symbol 4: Alan Watts 74

    Charging Symbol 4 75

    Symbol 5: Aleister Crowley 76

    Charging Symbol 5 78

    Symbol 6: Charles Bukowski 79

    Charging Symbol 6: 80

    Symbol 7: Terrence McKenna 81

    Charging Symbol 7 82

Symbol 8: Roy Eugene Davis 83

Charging Symbol 8 84

Appendix 1: Examples of Methods Used to Change State of Mind 86

Taoist Yoga Inner Smile 86

Cleaning you house, room or apartment 87

Russian coldwater dousing 87

Doing something stupid/incredibly childish 88

Voluntary Silence 89

6. Wolverine Walking/Contrarian Walking 89

Power Posing 90

Appendix 2: CHIR creation notes and other handwritten draft examples ... 91

Appendix 3: Origami/Masu Box Instructions 98

Endnotes 100

Illustrations 101

Recommended Reading/Bibliography 102

Occult and Psyhcology 102

Eastern Philosophy/Technique 104

Various Topics 104

Illustrations 106

ABOUT THE AUTHOR 108

Introduction

This is starting point and a simple how too guide regarding the understanding, creation/charging of and use of a magical sigils. While sigils exist abundantly in every culture, the average individual does not take into account how many exist and are at work in their everyday lives. These "Sigils" could also be referred to as visual mnemonic devices because in fact they are. In this book the term sigil will be loosely interchanged at times with the term sign or symbol. While not always linguistically or grammatically correct the assumption will be made that the reader understands what we are working with here.

Included are examples of ways to create sigils which range from simple to the more complex. Also you will find information on other elements which can be used in the creation of a sigil, brief bios of known and lesser known individuals and accounts/examples of the author's own experiences.

Sign: A display used to identify or advertise a place of business or a product

Sign: Something material or external that stands for or signifies something spiritual

Symbol: Something which stands for or suggests something else by reason of relationship, association, convention, or accidental resemblance; especially: a visible sign of something invisible <the lion is a symbol of courage>

(Definitions from *Merriam Webster* online dictionary)

A drive through the smallest town or city exposes one to countless symbols, sigils and hyper-sigils in the form of signage on the outside of gas stations, convenience stores, restaurants and businesses. One look at a trademarked sign (sigil) representing a brand can invoke all the energy of the past experiences ever involved with it. The food, atmosphere, events, costumed characters, commercials, jingles, cartoon art, and childhood birthday parties that are invoked by the sign or logo outside your favorite childhood restaurant are a good example.

Some sigils gain or lose power over time and take on entirely different meanings. At one point in history seeing the deaths head or Jolly Roger flag meant that you were soon to be dead. Today's Jolly Roger is affixed to party/recreational boats and part of children's films as if the original idea of giving no quarter and killing everyone had never been attached to it in the past. To fully grasp this imagine the signs and symbols of the terrorist organizations present in the world today (2013) being flown on the flags of a party boat on a lake 50 years from now.

An obvious example of a powerful and infamous sigil transforming is the swastika/sunwheel. Long before the existence of the Nazi party and the rise of Adolf Hitler, the swastika was used by various eastern religions to represent a sacred empowering force and was widely used as a religious symbol. (Endnote 1)

As the Nazi party formed with its roots deep in occult philosophy, it adopted the swastika as its symbol for the Aryan race. As a result, the swastika was charged with a great deal of negative energy lasting into the present day. More than sixty years after WWII and the fall of the Nazi party the swastika carries an infamously bad reputation in the western world.

Corporations, sports teams and governments use these sigils powerfully on a daily basis to influence you, and many times not in your best interest.

Why do these sigils/symbols/signs have such attractive qualities and the power to attract ones attention? Why have so many systems such as Jungian archetypes and the various in sets of tarot cards been created in attempt to understand them and put them to use? Why do the similar lines, images and themes appear throughout the history of mankind? While questions can be asked and theories developed about theses image one thing is certain; they have a profound influence and can be used to the advantage of the reader if wished.

Sigils are present and powerful aspects of daily life and can be better understood by anyone. They can be used for both high and low magic, memory recall and motivation. From achieving one's

> "If you know the enemy and know yourself you need not fear the result of a hundred battles." - Sun Tzu, *Art of War*

object of desire, to attempting regression into an atavistic state of universal conscious. (Endnote 2) With that being the case, I would propose that not only should they be understood but created, experienced and used by the willing and able reader.

It was said that in the ancient Olympic Games there were three types of people present. They were: The Competitors, the Observers and the Vendors. The use and understanding of sigil magic requires one to create, charge and put to use a sigil, not just sit on your ass and look for the next occult book to purchase. The time to compete is now.

Why do sigils work?

While this book is by no means a psychological, linguistic or religious analysis, the simple answers are WILL and EFFORT. Call it magic, mnemonics, hijacking a language system, the use of a sigil can and does work regardless of the labels applied.

Consider the following maxim in western magic:

To know, to dare, to will, to keep silent

The above is taken from Eliphas Levi's *The Doctrine of Ritual Magic* and is what Levi refers to as the four words of the magus. The sentence while taken out of context to a degree is the basic guideline for the execution of any successful operation magical or otherwise and can be broken down further:

TO KNOW: Seek the knowledge and proper method of doing

TO DARE: Venture beyond the certain. Go past the gate keepers which hold you back (e.g. Fear, tradition morality, belief systems, karmic concepts)

TO WILL: Have the ability, skill direction, momentum and guts to go forward with the action and effect the change.

TO KEEP SILENT: To not lessen, or destroy the outcome by speaking about it and investing excessive energy in the event or results.

To know that the works, and its outcome, are only tools the means to an end. Generally you do not mow the yard and then push the mower around with you for the rest of the day.

Without a doubt the personal use and creation of sigils is not for everyone. The value of using them as a tool will not easily be understood or accepted by everyone.

What you can do with this book

You may read this book and decide that everything within it is garbage and that is alright. You may take this book and add it to your growing collection of occult related topics while never attempting anything described in the contents and that too is quite alright. You might also be the one in a hundred readers who have the guts to see if any of this works which is more than alright. Many read, few remember, and even less act upon the knowledge they acquire. It is entirely up to you. This is a push...

Respectfully,

Vincent K Luce

Begin

Definitions from Merriam Webster online dictionary

SIGIL: 1: Seal, Signet

2: **A sign, word, or device to have occult power in magic**

Occult: 1: **To shut off from view**

Synonyms: Cloak, conceal, cover, disguise, enshroud, mask, obscure, hide, paper over, screen, shroud, suppress, veil.

Take a moment to review the above definitions and consider how you personally define the word OCCULT. When you hear the word spoken or see it written how do you feel about it? Does it give you a sense of excitement, evil, darkness or perhaps visions of people dressed in dark cloaks? What has led you to think what you do about the word OCCULT? Is it the result of direct experience, reading or inference as a result of real teachings? Or, is your perception of the word OCCULT based on what others have shoved down your throat, founded by the television, book and movie industry which has been spoon fed to you by popular culture since birth? Has some robotic asshole smashed his particular belief system into your psyche causing you to accept their definition of the word OCCULT without question?

Consider the idea that that word OCCULT has been manipulated and hijacked by popular media, confused members of religious institutions and weak worried minds. It somehow became the accepted one word mantra (sigil?) used to inspire fear and general distaste to anything it has been applied.

This popular misuse of the word OCCULT still goes unchallenged to this day and without a doubt you can thank such things as the Satanic Panic of the 1980s' (Disproven by FBI's Kenneth Lanning in his 1992 study) and a slew of entertaining movies like The Omen, The Exorcist and Rosemary's Baby (Which seem to be treated as factual events by some viewers.)

While entertaining and scary fodder for conversation these films and the media's portrayal of the OCCULT can soundly be called misleading and based on fear driven delusions.

What other things present in your life have been hijacked and used as one word banishing devices? Does the fact that sigil magic is considered possibly something from the OCCULT stop you from wanting to involve yourself in its use? Is your definition of the word and things associated with it simply part of the tools of a gate keeper who does not allow you to go any further?

IDISE by Emil Doepler

ONCE SAT WOMEN,

THEY SAT HERE, THEN THERE.

SOME FASTENED BONDS,

SOME IMPEDED AN ARMY,

SOME UNRAVELED FETTERS:

FLEE THE ENEMY!

- *First Mersberg Incantaion.* 10th century

Words of warning

When involving yourself in the study of anything Occult related or outside of the norm where you reside you may want to take into consideration how or if you should speak about what you are doing. Telling someone you are practicing magic, casting spells or invoking demons may have many and sometimes long term repercussions. This has nothing to do with your right to do whatever you want, when you want to; and everything to do with realizing that unless you are living the life of a hermit or truly seek to be ostracized, you need to gel with, to some degree, the society around you. Something even as integrated as the practice yoga is in western culture may draw sour responses from the uninformed.

The truth here being you can, and certainly will drive people in your life away if you go about the study of any topic improperly. Sigil Magic is a tool like any mnemonic device but on a bit deeper level. There is no reason for you to alienate yourself from the general populace with its use. That is why I would like you to consider the concept that you, by reading this booklet are in fact studying the art of Sigil Magic just as if you would study any other topic. That when you put a sigil to use you in fact are not casting a spell or cursing something as much as you are FOCUSING and MEDITATING upon it as you would :

An anchor in Neurolinguistic programming

A mantra or yantra from the Hindu/yogic traditions

A prayer or chant

A devotion to a Saint

A mnemonic device

A piece of art, religious or otherwise

A journal entry

A photograph that inspires emotions

> People will kill in the name of this idea that they have of the nature of reality. That is what it comes down to you know. People receive these ideas in childhood and thy never really question them. And not questioning an idea is a sign of an unconscious mentality. It is the sign of a mentality that has not fully woken up. - Graham Hancock (*Duncan Trussel Family Hour* podcast 7/3/13)

ROBERT ANTON WILSON
1932-2007

Robert Anton Wilson has been called a Philosopher, occultist, author, Discordian prophet/pope, PhD. in Psychology, guerrilla ontologist and more. Robert Anton Wilson wrote both fiction and non-fiction on a number of topics including logic, linguistics/structure of language, secret societies, conspiracy theories , Aleister Crowley, magic, yoga and Timothy Leary's 8 circuit model of consciousness to name a few.

In his lifetime Wilson claimed to have met with supernatural and other worldly creatures of all types and wrote about his experiences in The Cosmic

Trigger. His theories and concepts such as Maybe Logic, reality tunnels are some of his lasting trademarks.

The author would go as far as to recommend you put this book down and pick up Prometheus Rising and read it as soon as possible. Even better read it while eating a hotdog without a bun on Friday for extra benefit.

> *I am a human being; I consider nothing that is human alien to me.* ~ Greek poet Terence (195/185–159 BC)

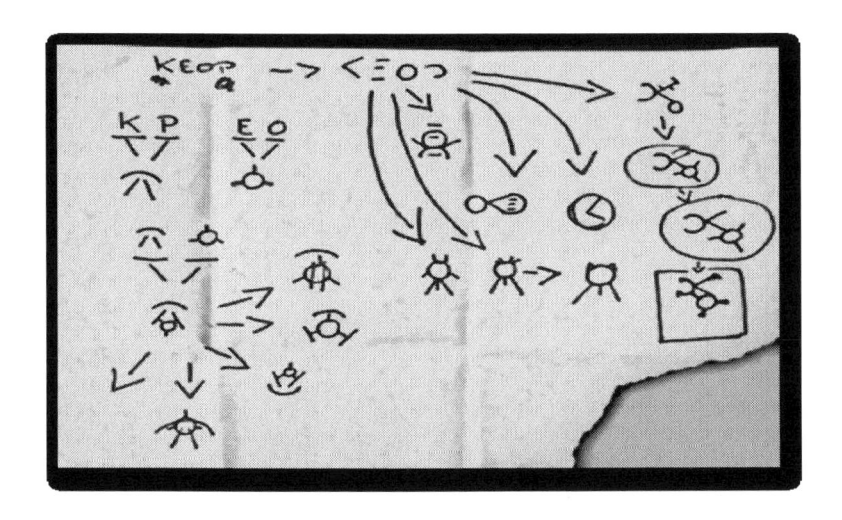

GIORDANO BRUNO

1548-1600

Dominican Friar, intellectual, philosopher, magician and heretic sentenced to death by the Roman inquisition for his controversial theories contrary to the Catholic doctrine. Giordano Bruno spread his ideas across Europe on a number of subjects including astrology, astronomy, mathematics, magic and the use of mnemonic devices. As a result he was excommunicated three times by the Catholic, Calvinist and Lutheran churches. Giordano Bruno's promoted theories which included the idea that sun was the center of the solar system and that each individual star was simply another sun with the ability to support life. His teachings left him consistently on the run, and eventually executed by Catholic inquisitors.

Giordano Bruno amongst his many works wrote *De Magica*, *Thesus De Magica*, and *De Imaginum, Signorum, Et Idearum Compostione* (*On the Compostion of Images,*

Signs and Ideas.) His work also included many mnemonic symbols and visual tools.

One of Giordano Bruno's mnemonic devices

Giordano Bruno was turned over by an unhappy student/patron to the Roman Inquisition and refused to recant his sacrosanct philosophies. Some of the charges brought against Bruno were:

Speaking against the church and its representatives

Opinions against the trinity, Christ and incarnation

Holding contrary opinions regarding the virginity of Mary

The practice of magic

On January 20, 1600, Bruno was declared a heretic and burned at the stake for his failure to recant before his inquisitors.

What is the Method Used?

In Austin Osman Spare's *The Book of Pleasure* he writes:

"Sigils are the monograms of thought, for the governments of energy (all heraldry, crests, monograms, are Sigils and the Karmas they govern), relating to Karma; a mathematical means of symbolizing desire and giving it form that has the virtue of preventing any thought and association on that particular desire (at the magical time), escaping the detection of the Ego, so that it does not restrain or attach such desire to its own transitory images, memories and worries, but allows its free passage into the subconscious."

In short the foundation of the basic method described within is:

1. IDENTIFY YOUR DESIRE
2. ENCAPSULATE DESIRE IN WRITING
3. TRANSFORM SENTENCE INTO A SIMPLE FORM EASILY VISUALIZED
4. ALLOW THE SYMBOLIZED DESIRE TO ENTER THE SUBCONSCIOUS (CHARGING)
5. ACHIEVE RESULTS

Also you do not have to dress up as a traditional magician, wizard or priest, build expensive temples, obtain virgin parchment, black goat's blood, etc., etc., in fact no theatricals or humbug. - A.O. SPARE, *The Book of Pleasure*

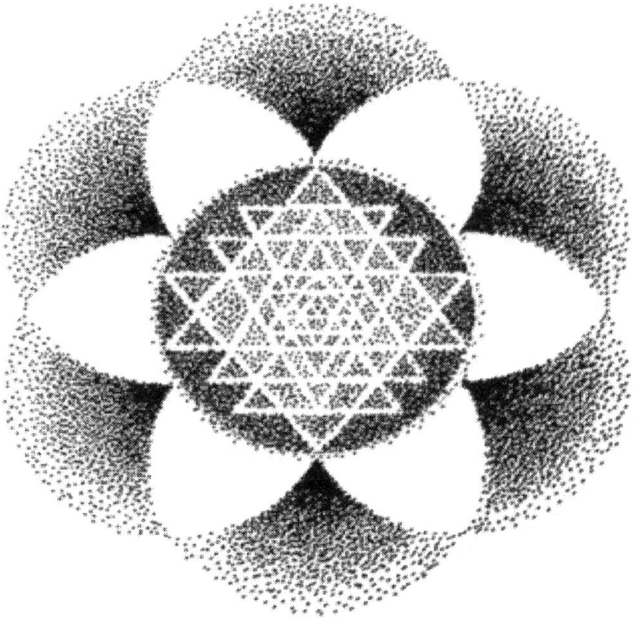

Getting Started...

Step One - Determining you goal

It is first important to ask the question "What is my sigil to be used for". What is the goal you hope to achieve and is it already obtainable by regular or mundane means? As interesting as taking the time to create and charge a magical sigil may be, is the act of doing so only a means for you to avoid doing to real work that must be done to achieve your goal? Think of what you can do without a sigil first to reach your goal and if you find those options are exhausted the creation of a sigil may be in order.

To begin you must first establish the goal in your mind and formulate it into a simple sentence of intention/desire. Keeping it brief is key and also helps to make things easier unless you consider the possibility of a very large written statement as part of the charging of the sigil itself. Lack of brevity may be an indication of poor organization/direction in most cases.

Bruce Lee once wrote this about the martial art of *Jeet Kune Do*: "In JKD, …. one does not accumulate but eliminate. It is not daily increase but daily decrease. The height of cultivation always runs to simplicity."

The formulation of your sentence of intention is where the boiling down of the sigil begins.

Here are some examples of sentences of intention:

1. It is my wish to get into better physical shape
2. I want to move on from my failing relationship. OR: I am seeking better relationships
3. I will have a more positive outlook on life

4. I will focus on a new path
5. I would like to maintain my motivation to complete this book
6. I would like to attract _____(Money, Opportunity, Love etc.)
7. Stay out of my way

Once you have developed your sentence of intention you will need to read it to yourself several times. Again review everything you could possibly do with the current personal and worldly resources available. Also consider how achieving this goal will fit into your life and if it is truly reasonable.

> If man could have half his wishes, he would double his troubles. – *Poor Richards Almanac*

While you set the limits of what you can truly accomplish it is important to remember there are limits which differ from person to person.

Consider the following again:

Are you seeking the goal for destructive or constructive purposes?

Is this goal within my reach, just out of my grasp, or ridiculous?

Have I focused on the normal path a person would take to achieve this goal and failed?

Am I doing this just to appear special or spooky to someone or to use it as a topic of conversation?

In some cases special attention is given to the sentence being written positively as opposed to negative. Does it matter to you? Some would argue that your statements of intention should always be positive. There is quite a difference between the following two sentences:

I am tired of being an overweight, out of shape slug.

I would like to do everything in my power to obtain my goal weight.

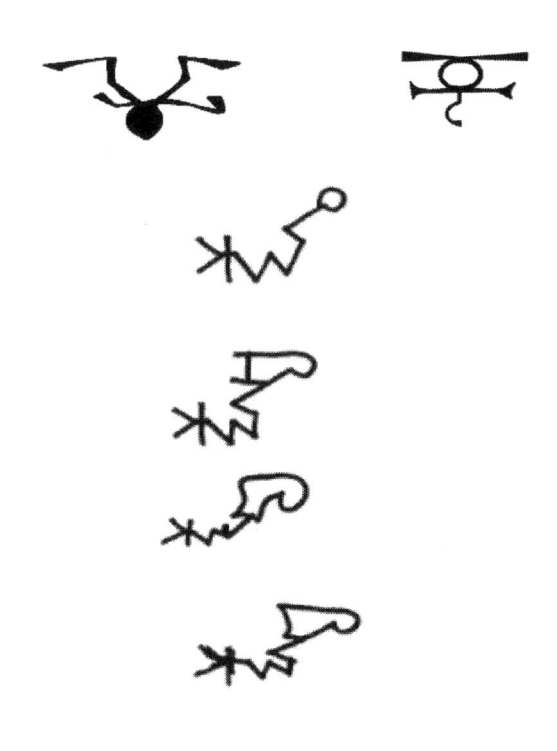

Step Two - Working with your sentence of intention

This is the point where you begin the ritual of creating the sigil. Take a moment to look up the word RITUAL. Ritual, like the word OCCULT tends to get people riled up thanks to popular culture's misuse of the word and the connotations placed upon it. Just because the word is abused and misused by so many does not mean that the concept of a ritual should not be of use to you. The negative views applied to the word ritual serve once again as gatekeepers driving the easily frightened away.

If you have any apprehension about the use of ritual think about the pregame actions some of your favorite athletes complete before they enter the field, course or ring. Be it a wearing a favorite shirt, completing a certain action prior to the start of a sporting event or simply saying a prayer before competing. Like sigils, rituals are part of everyday life. You can also simply reframe it all by using terms like formulating, fabricating or any other word synonymous with creation.

Using a sigil is not the average means of approaching a goal so why should its creation be average? The most basic tools for creating a sigil are a pen and paper. Even in these early stages importance can be assigned to the pen and paper used in writing your sentence of intention if you wish. Using a special pen (e.g. with the name, emblem or color of something related to your goal) and paper is a good example. Always remember you are undertaking a ritual that is intended to have a strong impact on your mind and world and every step from this point on matters.

Examples:

- ❖ Using a pen or writing device related to your goal.

- ❖ Paper with significant colors related to goal or somehow related to it.
- ❖ Setting/place where you do the work/create the sigil. A location that might put you in a specific state of mind congruent with your goal.
    1. Your own quite place or room
    2. In the a very busy area crowded by people (if chaos is needed)
    3. A place of significance to influence the required mood
    4. Near the location of the goal you wish to achieve (e.g. the union hall of the college you are trying to get accepted to).
- ❖ Changing or affecting mindset(aka Set) : Changing your mindset to one of extreme calm or high excitement(Consciously or emotionally) by:
    1. Food or lack of. After a large meal or after eating food specific to your goal.
    2. Coffee, herbal teas, caffeine (other state changing foods/drinks)
    3. Intense exercise or its polar opposite.
    4. Meditation (Mantra, Yantra, one pointed concentration, Metta)
    5. Sex or lack of.
    6. Music ranging from white noise, binaural beats, sounds in nature, classical, acoustic, bubblegum pop, rock metal, death metal, to complete audio dissonance.
    7. Smells/Odors. From good to bad. Lavender and cinnamon and many others for example are documented to have a very positive effect on the mind. One extreme example of this is an unverified story of a band member

who reportedly kept a rotted crow carcass on tour with him and would smell it to get into the proper mindset before a show (Always keep in mind your own personal health in safety).
8. Anything that would invoke strong emotions or energy.

(See Appendix 1 for more state/mindset changing ideas)

The use of these special tools, settings and mindsets are the real beginning of energizing and charging your sigil.

Take for example all that is involved in a professional football team's logo which is in reality highly charged sigil. In one team logo alone you have the following things consistently giving it momentum:

- ❖ Parent to son/daughter familiarity with the team (Like or dislike)
- ❖ Hours of watching the team play, hours of listening to commentators during and outside the game, hours of discussion with family and friends (sometimes very heated and passionate)
- ❖ Unfulfilled personal dreams on several levels vicariously fantasized and observed through the game and its players. (Athletic achievement, wealth, fame, popularity/attraction.)
- ❖ Deep emotions felt during wins and losses on both a personal and group level.
- ❖ The emotional investment made in following the lives of the players who go through ups and downs in their professional and personal lives which in turn creates yet another avenue for the fan to live vicariously through them.

Step Three - Boiling down your sentence of intent

1: Create the sentence of intent (Containing your goal or ambition).

In this case the goal is to avoid and remove unwanted interaction with someone in your life. The sentence of intent I will work with as an example is:

STAY OUT OF MY WAY

2: Apply a method of dissolving/boiling the sentence down. In this example I have decided to remove every vowel and every duplicate letter. While this is one way to go about it, it is not the only way and finding your own or other methods is encouraged strongly. Other ideas will be addressed later.

STAY OF MY WAY

Becomes: **ST~~AY~~ ~~OUT~~ ~~OF~~ M~~Y~~ W~~AY~~**

Leaving us with this to work with: **STFMW**

3: Begin to combine the remaining letters into a symbol/glyph

The letters **STFMW** were broke down manipulated into two symbols

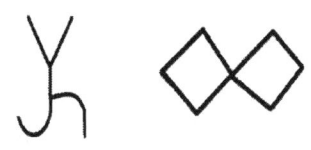

4: Draw and combine what is left freely and with the use of any device artistic/symbolic or other as you wish

The above symbols were then combined resulting in the following

5: I then continued to work with the symbol and came out with the end result of

This symbol is now ready to be charged.

Step Four - Charging the sigil

Once you have designed your sigil created it sits holding some of the energy drawn into it during the creation. This is the time to put some real heat on (In) it, adding intensity to allow it a special place in your psyche. To make it matter, to allow it to be burned/frozen into your conscious and subconscious mind while stopping the internal dialogue long enough to embed the sigil.

Charging the sigil is also the point where you can chose to, if only for moment take what you are doing and slow the observation of reality down. Much like frames per second in a movie, you can purposely go from 50 frames to 100 or more. An example of this occurring would be the detailed memory one has after a head on car crash or other world stopping incident. After such an event, many times the victim can remember very fine details of the accident scene for a long time.

Charging the sigil can be as intense and intricate or as low key and boring as you wish. What matters is if the ritual or method your chose has the ability to imprint the sigil in your mind. Some simple methods of charging are as follows and descend from high intensity to low. They are to be done while focusing on the desired sigil.

1. Intense physical exertion (exercise, sex, work)
2. Placing yourself in situations which induce fear and adrenaline
3. Purposely placing one's self in an intense or uncomfortable situation. Doing things out of character or contrary to your general lifestyle/personality/reality tunnel.

4. Seeking experiences outside of your personal, cultural or moral norms (e.g. a football player taking ballet)
5. Intense and detailed recall of memories (good or bad) with focus on the energy evoked.
6. Calm, focused meditation upon the goal and sigil (E.g. Vispana/one pointed meditation) or achievement, seeking what A.O. Spare referred to as a state of VACUITY.
7. Abstinence from some aspect of your life (Exercise, sex, pleasure)
8. Attempting to visualize or encounter the aspects of your sigil in a dream.
9. Ritual (Social, Magical, Self-Created, etc.)
10. Public Ceremony (e.g. graduation ceremony to empower a diploma)
11. Wank method as described by Grant Morrison in his article *Pop Magic* from *Disinformation: The Book of Lies*. (Endnote 4)
12. Focus on sigil at a very low point or time of despair.(Endnote 5)

Specific Examples of Charging

1. Create sigil and while focusing on it do an exercise called the 90/90/90 which involves sitting against a wall at a 90 degree angle with your knees bent at a 90 degree angle for 90 seconds.
2. Create sigil and then embark on doing something you have never done before. This could be as simple as taking a different way to get somewhere familiar or involving yourself in an activity you would not normally do. Penjak Silat instructor Herman Suwanda advised that stepping off the beaten path was very important to ones development and could be achieved by something as simple as simple as switching the

order in which you go to the bathroom (defecate before urinating or vice versa).

3. Create sigil and later in the day go to an instructional class based on White Magic. Speak boldly about topics contrary to White Magic such as anything related to what may be considered Black Magic (e.g. Church of Satan or Voodoo) and see where the conversation goes. A similar example would be to speak to a sports fan negatively about his favorite team. People in reality do this type of energizing all the time and use the US vs. THEM argument to re-establish membership in their tribal groupings.

4. Create a state of mind or emotion related to your sigil by replicating others who have sought out and achieved goals similar to your sentence of intention. For example, if you are a mixed martial art competitor you would study the mindset and training attitudes of other successful fighters and attempt a healthy replication of it. Watching training videos, fights and interviews involving the fighter of your choice an making a conscious attempts to replicate or model (Neurolinguistic Programming style) would be a good example. Fictional movies can motivate and invoke the mindset needed and that is why films like Rocky (for boxers) and Vision Quest (for wrestlers) work well.

5. Create your sigil and then get a massage. Focus on this sigil as long as possible while doing so.

Crows Foot/ Witches Foot

Unity

Destruction/ Disorder

Sign of Hermes Variation

Winter

The Family Man with his Wife and Children

Adaptations from Rudolph Koch's Book of Signs

A Second Method of Sigil Creation

AS DESCRIBED BY DISCORDION LEGIONAIRE KEOP72

STEP 1: Write out your statement of intent.

   STAY HEALTHY

STEP 2: Put all of the vowels at the end of the statement

   STHLTHAYEAY

STEP 3: Reverse the order

   YAEYAHTLHTS

```
A  B  C  D  E  F  G  H  I  J  K  L  M  N  O  P  Q  R  S  T  U  V  W  X  Y  Z
1  2  3  4  5  6  7  8  9 10 11 12 13 14 15 16 17 18 19 20 21 22 23 24 25 26
```

  YAEYAHTLHTS Becomes 25-1-5-25-1-8-20-20-12-8-19

STEP 5: Put into Numerical Order

   1-1-5-8-8-12-19-20-20-25-25

STEP 6: Convert back to letters

AAEHHLSTTYY

STEP 7: Place letters in a square grid. If you are left an uneven amount leave empty space in grid.

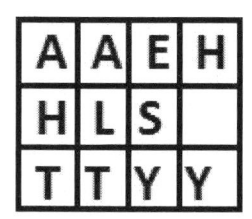

A	A	E	H
H	L	S	
T	T	Y	Y

STEP 8: Chose a number corresponding to the number of squares you have made either vertically or horizontally. In this case the number is 4 taken from the horizontal. 4 will be the number of moves made on the grid to create the base form of the sigil. Now place a dark circle over any one of the vowels in the grid. From that vowel draw a line to the consonant of your choice and place a dark circle over it. Again draw a line to the vowel of your choice and place a dark circle over it. Finally draw a line to the next vowel and place a dark circle over it. The symbol made by this process is the base from which you can now work with.

For and end result of:

43

Base for sigil

The base for the sigil can then be used as is, cleaned up or developed from this point as you wish or not considering the complete lack of rules required by the goddess Eris. This method is purposely ridiculous.

Anagram to Symbol Method

This method involves the use of anagrams which are changed into symbols. The symbols are then combined to create a sigil.

Beginning with your statement of intent/desire:

Increased Cardio

Take your statement of intent and re-arrange it into an anagram. You can do this on your own but to save time and have multiple options it is easier to place the statement into an online anagram generator (easily found and available on multiple sites). Increased Cardio when placed into an anagram generator comes up with many variations. I chose:

NICER ACID ADORES

I then took the anagram and turned each word into a related symbol. In this case NICER became a smile, ACID became a + sign per the PH balance of acid, and ADORES easily transformed into a heart.

∪ + ♡

The new symbols were then combined as follows to create the sigil for Increased Cardio.

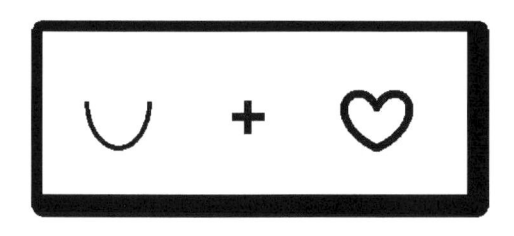

Combined into:

The sigil is finalized as:

Meanings behind the symbols within The Knight, Death and the Devil

THE KNIGHT, DEATH AND THE DEVIL
ALBRECHT DURER 1517

A breakdown of a hypersigil

The Knight, Death and the Devil have been explained several ways and the following is based on my recount of a lecture given by Dr Paul Whitsell. The purpose of this is to explore what depth the picture has and the use of it as a hypersigil. This is only one of the many interpretations which exist.

The Knight: Battle worn and surrounded by death, evil and apathy surround him yet he remains stern and solid facing forward riding onto his fate.

The Horse is also aged and worn from combat but remains reliable

A dog which runs alongside the knight ever faithful representing the friends and family which stay with one through thick and thin.

Death riding before the knight on a dying horse. Holding the hourglass that counts the time until the knight's eventual death.

Headstone and nearby skull also signifying and reminding the knight of the certainty of death before him. Headstone contains the initials of the artist and year of the piece.

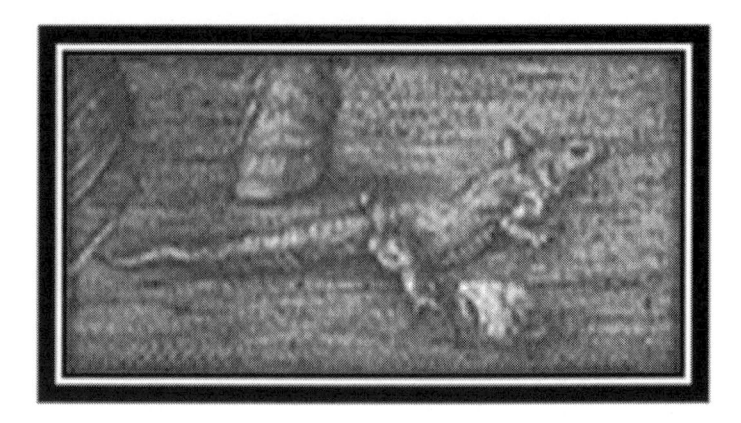

The lizard lying beneath the horse representing another form of evil near the knight as he rides.

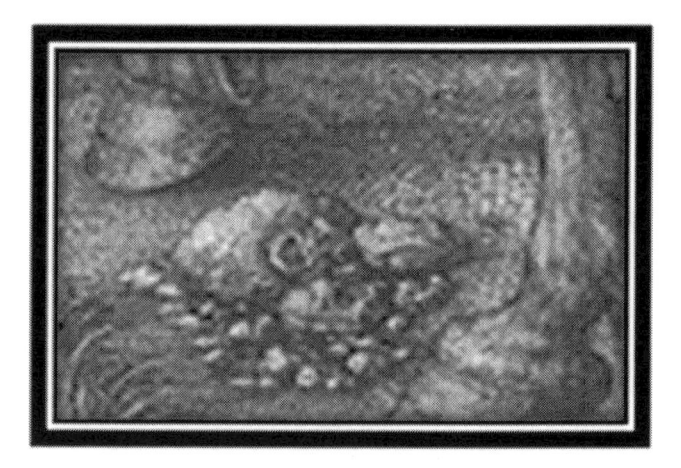

A pile of shit which the knight's horse will step in representing the always present problems in the life of the knight.

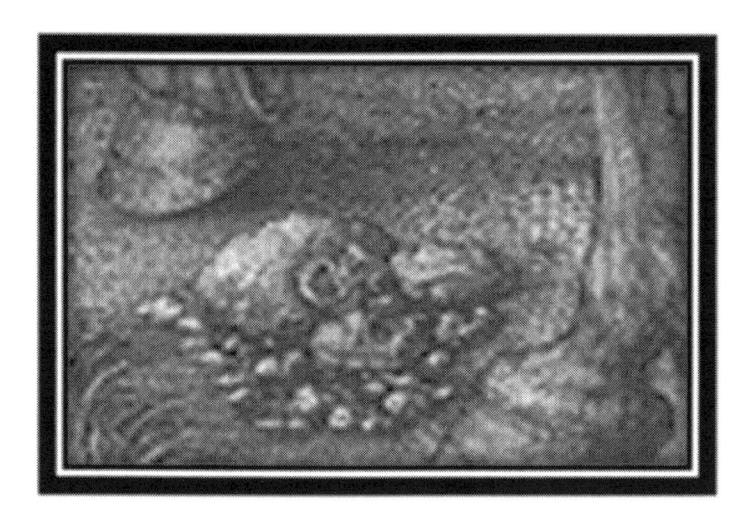

The lance of the knight which is wrapped in animal fur. The tail/fur was reported to leave more humane wounds and represents the knight's mercy to his enemy.

The Devil standing near tempting the knight towards evil as he travels along his path. The lance of the devil which is viciously barbed so that once it hooks you it will keep you and injure (Unlike the lance of the knight).

The city off far in the distance which the knight protects but is not quite able to live in. It is far away and represents the fact that it flourishes and is protected by the knight while he remains outside of it surrounded by evil and in combat to do so.

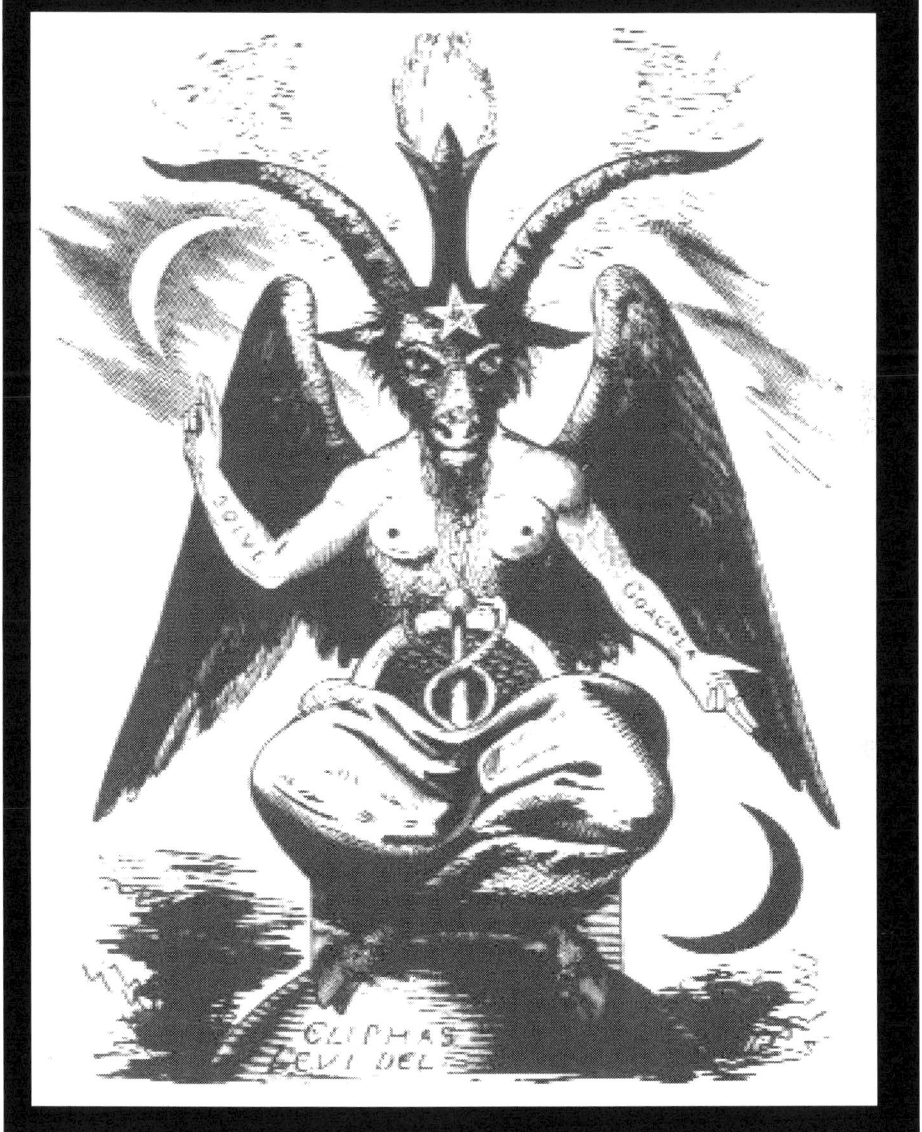
SOLVE
COAGULA
ELIPHAS
LEVI DEL.

Eliphas Levi's Sabbatical Goat
Sigil of Baphomet

Breakdown of Sigil Elements

1. Head: Element of fire

2. Wings: Element of air

3. Scales: Element of water

4. Legs: Element of earth

5. Pentagram on forehead representing human intelligence

6. Breasts: Hermaphroditic characteristic, or the divine androgyne.

7. Goat face/Face of the Goat of Mendes thought to be the goat of the witches Sabbath

8. Caduceus/Wand: The union of the sexes

9. White and black moons: Good and Evil

10. Torch: Divine revelation

11. "SOLVE" (Dissolve) on right arm, "COAGULA" (Combine) on left arm: Reference the alchemical maxim SOLVE ET COAGULA (Dissolve and combine). The dissolution of man's outer ego/karma forces which keep him from his true self and to then combine to form a new integrated self/rebirth.

According to Eliphas Levi this sigil can be understood on three different levels

1. The folkloric devil

2. Male sexuality

3. The astral light

This is but one of several interpretations of this sigil.

Creating a sigil/Charging Box

A sigil charging box is something which came about as the result of using origami as a form of mediation.

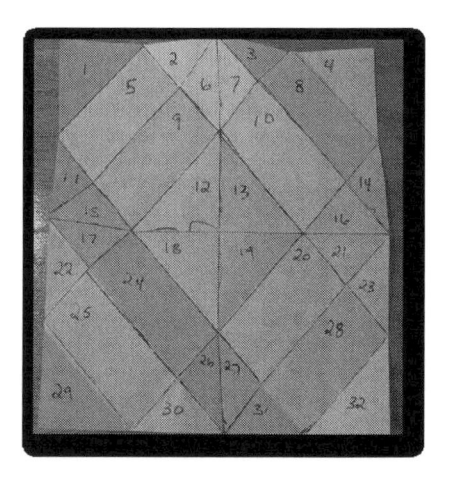

While folding an origami (or masu box) is not very hard to do, folding boxes which are visually appealing and geometric is a bit more challenging. While folding countless boxes I began to see their possibly application for sigils and other aspects of magic.

I saw that the folds made in the creation of an origami box made many separated surfaces and segments which are later combined to make the final product. These segments (differing in number based on the method which the box is folded) and surfaces were observed to be excellent places to combine various sigils and related symbols with the final outcome being a Sigil Device or Charging Box.

APE OF THOTH BOX

The charging box itself can be used for many things. Some examples are:

A three dimensional log of your personal sigils

A charging station for future sigils

An altar or personal Puja (Hindu)

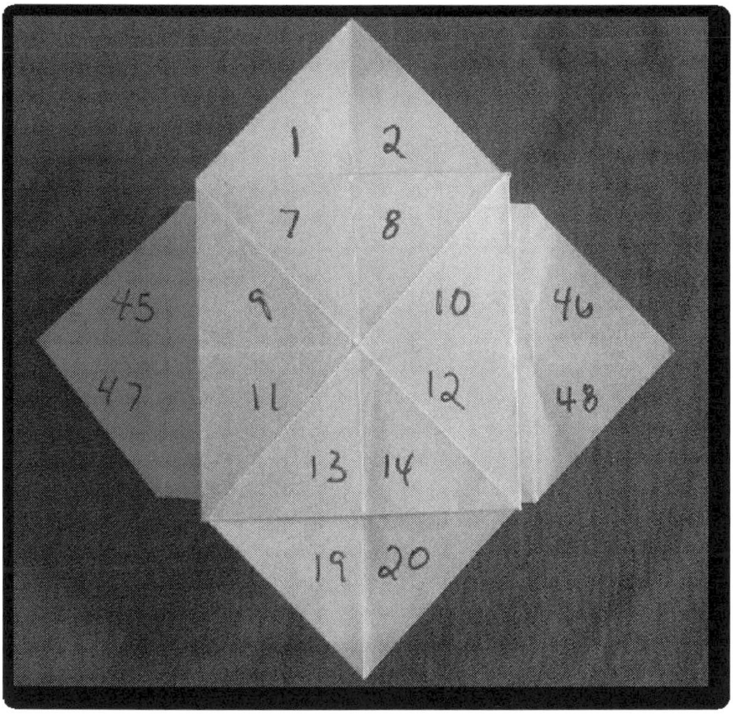
1
2
7
8
45
9
10
46
47
11
12
48
13
14
19
20

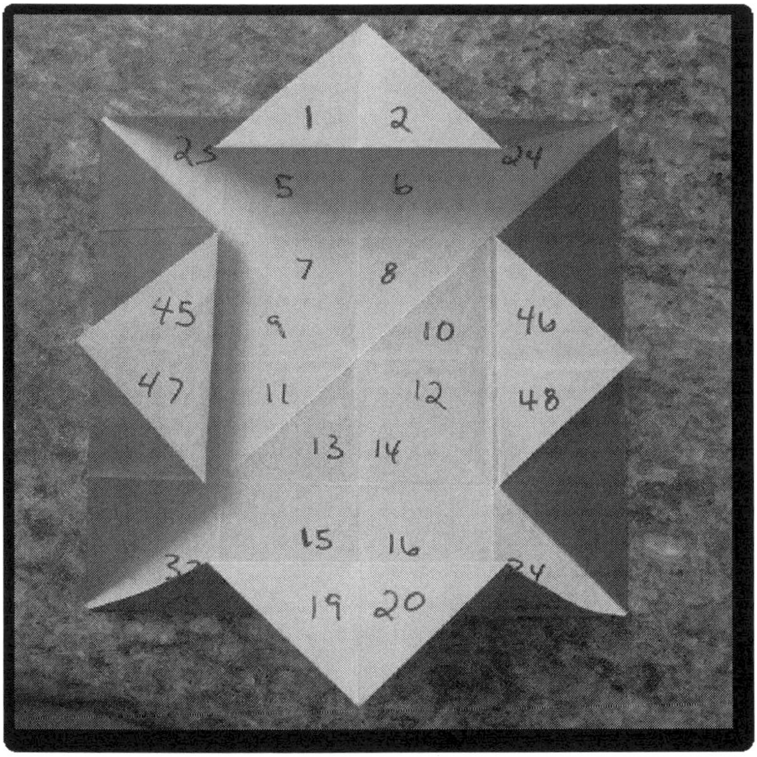
1
2
25
24
5
6
7
8
45
9
10
46
47
11
12
48
13
14
15
16
19
20

Unfolded Sigil Box

The Sigil Device/ Charging Box has been included here as an example of taking the creation of sigils a bit further. To show how the use of sigils can go in a more individual direction and evolve (or devolve).

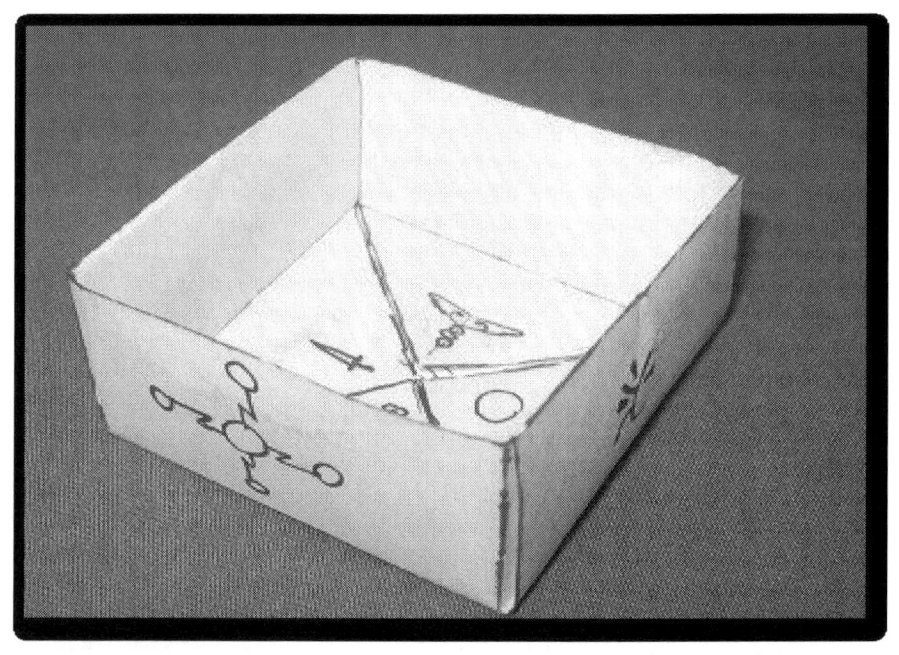

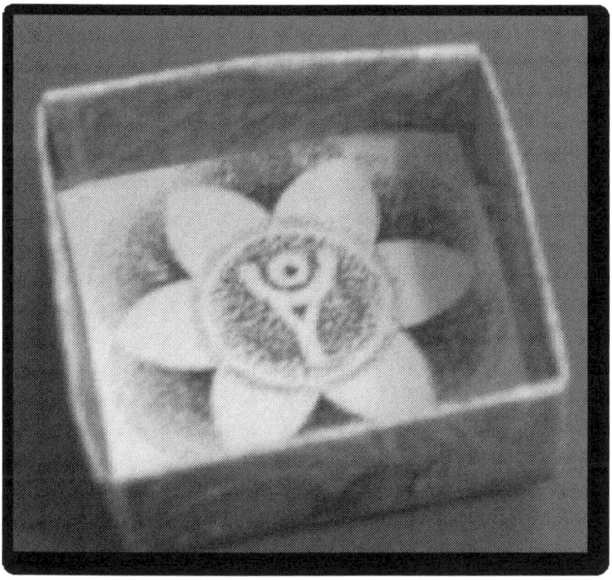

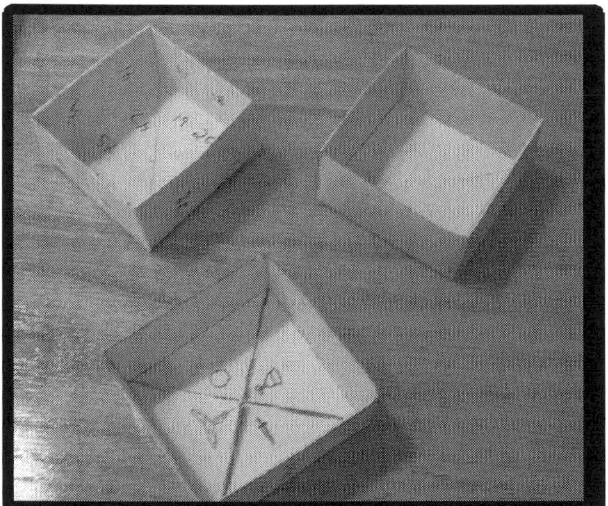

What to do with unused, old, no longer needed sigils

While the answer is: Whatever you want to do with them, a small out take from the Hagakure might also shed light on this:

"In the Kamigata area they have a sort of tiered lunch box they use for a single day when flower viewing. Upon returning, they throw them away, trampling them underfoot. As might be expected, this is one of my recollections of the capital [Kyoto]. The end is important in all things."

The Hagakure (The book of the Samurai)

CHIR Hypersigil

Creating the Chapel of the Infinite Reader (CHIR)
An Example of a Hypersigil Creation

The Chapel of the Infinite Reader is a hypersigil developed for the invocation of a personal mindset I wished to create representing times of intense or enduring study/reading. It is positive space within my own head. A space filled with creative intent which might possibly be accessed through the hyprsigil. The idea was first hand drawn and then given to a professional artist to re-interpret and complete. (See Appendix 2 for the actual hand drawn process.)

CHIR started with the culmination of eight influential authors in my life. Author's whose work in the past had repeated positive influence.

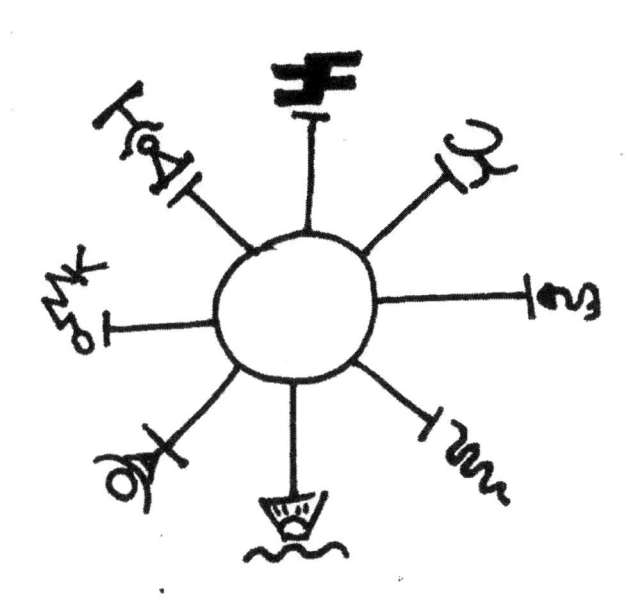

They are the following eight:

1. Joseph Campbell (American mythologist, writer and lecturer)
2. J. Krishnamurti (Indian speaker and writer on philosophical/spiritual topics)
3. Ram Dass (American contemporary spiritual teacher and author)
4. Alan Watts (Philosopher, writer, and speaker, best known as an interpreter and who popularized Eastern philosophy for a Western audience)

5. Aleister Crowley (Occultist, mystic, ceremonial magician, poet and mountaineer, who was responsible for founding the religious philosophy of Thelema)
6. Charles Bukowski (Alcoholic, poet, novelist and short story writer)
7. Terence McKenna (Ethnobotanist, philosopher, psychonaut, researcher, teacher, lecturer, and writer)
8. Roy Eugene Davis (Teacher of Kriya Yoga, Yogi and author)

The center of CHIR contains the image of the Sri-Yantra.

The Sigils and their Creation

Symbol 1: Joseph Campbell

Joseph Campbell was a prolific reader and autodidact. His work in comparative mythology and the structure of myth is without comparison. As the letters of the sigil involving Joseph Campbell's name began to develop I saw the letters taking the shape of books and went with it. The final sigil became a view from above at books standing staggered next to each other.

Charging Symbol 1:
Considering the amount of reading involved in Joseph Campbell's life and study of various cultural myths and legends I decided to study a group of people very foreign to myself and studied them for several weeks. I chose the Rastafarai (Rastafarian movement). I read several books on the Rastafari culture and way of life. I also watched the documentary Roaring Lion which gave a concise

history of the movement. I also spent one week with work radio set to the Sirius/XM reggae channel THE JOINT which was interesting because I generally don't enjoy that style of music. One result of this study was the realization that the likelihood of running into a true Rastafarian representative in Northern America is unlikely. Despite that fact the rastifarian culture and has had a very obvious effect on music, art and even to a degree philosophy since its birth. This somewhat fell under the charging of the Crowley symbol as well in that it involved approaching something very foreign to me.

Symbol 2: J. Krishnamurti

J. Krishnamurti was a speaker and writer on spiritual and philosophical subjects. His work covered such topics as meditation, fear, the nature of man and psychological revolution. As a small boy he was discovered by and raised by members of the Theosophical Society to become world teacher. He eventually rejected that idea, disbanded the organization involved in his development and went on the rest of his life to teach and speak publically on a number of topics.

While I was boiling the name down into a sigil I saw the lines leading to simply into a stylized letter K and left it that way.

Charging symbol 2

Read more of J. Krishnamurti's work. Make an attempt to understand how it may or may not apply to my life. Also take into account Krishnamurti's rather unusual upbringing.

Symbol 3: Ram Dass

After studying Kriya yoga for a short time I ran again into a reoccurring name that I had seen for several years. In the past I would see the name Ram Dass or a photograph of him and almost every time I would have a negative feeling. I would always think "Who is this asshole?" and pass by any further inquiry.

Later I had began listening to a podcast called The Duncan Trussell Family Hour (Previously called The Lavender Hour) and the host Duncan Trussell would continuously mention Ram Dass and a book written by him titled *Be Here Now*. I read *Be Here Now* and found that it explained yoga in a way that was much easier for me to grasp. Amazingly enough Ram Dass lectures became available online (*Be Here Now Podcast* by with host Raghu Markus) and I have been very influenced by his teachings since.

While working with his name and turning it into a sigil form I manipulated the remaining RMDS into what in my mind's eye looked like a snake in a basket. I then used that to form a snake (kundalini energy?) rising from a basket.

Charging Symbol 3
Study the Hanuman Chalisa which is a hymn devoted to the Hindu deity Hanuman. Devote one entire meditation session to

focusing on Hanuman. Focus on and eventually understand why saying the name Hanuman out loud is believed by some be able to exorcise demons and ghosts.

Symbol 4: Alan Watts

British-born writer and philosopher, Watts was best known for interpreting and making popular Eastern philosophy and Buddhism for a Western audience. I was introduced to Watt's writing by a roommate and found *The Book (On the Taboo Against Knowing Who You are)* to be intriguing.

For some reason while boiling down this sigil it began to take on the shape of a snake similar to the sigil for used to represent Ram Dass.

Charging Symbol 4

I began to take the study of Buddhism seriously and started to attend a Buddhist temple to mediate. I made somewhat of a cold call to a Buddhist Sri Lankan/Thai temple and was lucky enough to be met by very nice people who were the caretakers of the facility. The mediation sessions began with long sessions of chanting. The attempt to follow and chant in the very foreign language alone while trying not to babble was a challenge. Chanting is followed by meditation focused on the breath. This also has led to considerable study of Buddhist teaching and Dharma.

In the process of charging this symbol I read many different articles on Alan Watts which led me to one by Professor/Psychologist Stanley Krippner titled *The Psychedelic Adventures of Alan Watts*. The article included detailed elements of Watts' alcoholism near the end of his life and that he was even in the process of seeking help for it shortly before his death.

Symbol 5: Aleister Crowley

So much has been and can be said about Aleister Crowley. He held many infamous titles such as The Wickedest Man Alive, To Mega Therion and the The Great Beast. Crowley left a very lasting magical legacy and impression on society and human psychology. The highs and lows of his life were many, Chess master, expert mountain climber, millionaire, adventurer, prolific writer, magician, leader, prophet, publically hated, financially destitute and heroin addict to name a few.

Multiple accounts of his life by biographers, sycophants, documentarians, musicians, psychonauts and the press have painted very intense and often dark image. His influence was wide spread and included a Harvard psychologist, cult leaders, a rocket scientist and slew of musicians.

In elementary school I began to read occult related material such as the *Man, Myth and Magic* encyclopedia series. As I read more and more occult related material I repeatedly ran into accounts and sometimes enthralling photographs of Crowley. I did not understand much of what I read at the time but found it usually frightening. Over the next twenty years of reading and research my opinions of Crowley changed and I saw him as very complex, both good and bad and possibly beyond dualism itself at times. I may never full understand the man, his work or his myth but consider much of his work influential and inspiring.

While working with Crowley's name I began to form it into sun rays and a variation of an Egyptian sun disk. Ending with the sun disc as symbol emanating knowledge downwards.

Charging Symbol 5

I looked into the possibility of joining the nearest Ordo Temples Orientalis (Also known as O.T.O.) group near my home town. The O.T.O. appeared to be the most legitimate group surviving to carry on Crowley's work and teachings. After a bit of looking into it though I ran into a dead end and stopped my pursuit of membership. My attempt to join could only be described at best: Half assed.

I decided that I would charge the symbol by learning to write out the law of Thelema with my left hand. The results were visually interesting. I also read *The Book of Law* for the first time along with the Concise Aleister Crowley by Richard Kaczynski.

> DO WHAT THOU WILT SHALL BE THE WHOLE OF THE LAW

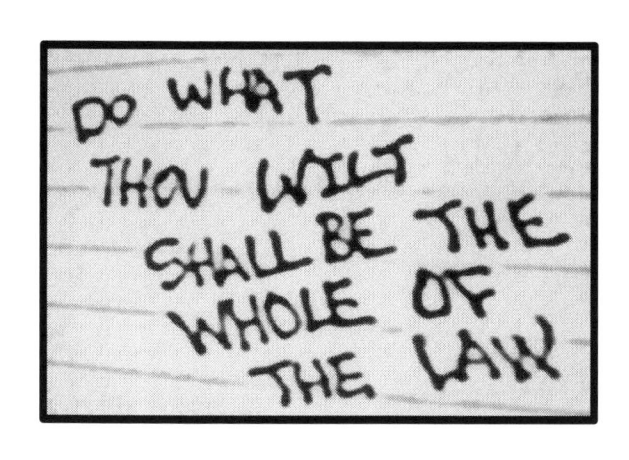

Symbol 6: Charles Bukowski

Charles Bukowski was very harsh individual, alcoholic and a prolific writer. He wrote numerous poems, short stories and novels which delved into the dirty dark side of humanity, alcohol and relationships. His stories and novels like *Ham on Rye and Post Office* were unlike anything else I had read before in my early 20's. While I am personally uncertain how much of his work was based on truth or fiction, his writing had a very powerful attitude and spoke many times for the enduring underdog.

When working with the letters in Charles Bukowski's name I decided that because he was such a buck the system/underdog type I would keep the vowels in his name to work with and wipe out all the consonants. Remaining was AEIOU which was then formed into a defiant man standing bolding with his arms raised in the air which seemed to deserve the name THE MAN WHO WILL FIGHT.

Charging Symbol 6:
Contemplate Charles Bukowski and his life. Sell my remaining Charles Bukowski books (*Post Office, Ham on Rye, Women, Hot*

Water Music, Tales of Ordinary Madness) and conclude that I had enough of him and his writing.

Symbol 7: Terrence McKenna

Terence Mckenna was an ethnobotoanist, explorer, psychonaut, evolutionary theorist, author and lecturer. His lectures, many of which are available in several locations online cover a wide range of topics including history, linguistics, magic, alchemy, and psychedelic drug use. He is known for his novelty theory based on the I Ching and which corresponded with the 2012 Mayan end of the world (Which truly shit the bed in 2012 fortunately) and the Stoned Ape theory of human evolution. While many of his theories have been pointed out as flawed even by his own brother Dennis McKenna, I have gained insight and information from his lectures. Also the almost hypnotic pacing of his speech is unlike anyone I have ever heard before. (Endnote 6)

While working with his name the letters seemed to work themselves into a relatively simple symbol by changing the angles of the letters. (Endnote 7)

Charging Symbol 7

This symbol was charged with the closest thing to psychedelic experience I could take part in without the use of drugs, a floatation tank. I did one hour in a floatation tank and it was a very pleasant experience. During the sensory deprivation I observed images of animals, heard random and sometimes not so random sounds, conversations and music and an intense moment of contemplation regarding the nature of fear and anger. I exited the tank feeling very refreshed and with a deep relaxation which almost brought me to tears.

Symbol 8: Roy Eugene Davis

Roy Eugene Davis is a spiritual teacher in the Kriya Yoga tradition and was ordained by Paramahansa Yogananda. Davis has taught Kriya Yoga for over 60 years and heads the Center For Spiritual Awareness. He has also published a multitude of books on Kriya Yoga which have been translated into 10 different languages. Davis's system of yoga was the first in which I began to meditate in and have a great respect for it.

Charging Symbol 8

Create and stick to a meditation schedule. Finish reading Autobiography of a Yogi

Appendix 1: Examples of Methods Used to Change State of Mind

All the following have been used or tried by the author. They are not for everyone and the author would like you to consider them for information purposes only.

Taoist Yoga Inner Smile

This technique is very simple and falls almost under the category of sympathetic magic. It is very simple to do and it works. It is a great way to get into a positive state of mind and body.

To complete the inner smile find a comfortable place or anywhere you will not be bothered and begin to smile. Attempt to make the smile as sincere as possible. Sometimes the mere act of beginning to do the Inner Smile seems so silly that you will find that you are legitimately smiling. You then imagine the energy and the warmth generated by the smile traveling down into your chest and organs.

For more information on detailed methods look for almost any book of Taoist exercises by Mantak Chia and you will find more instruction on the Inner Smile (Usually near the front) or get his complete book on the subject.

Cleaning you house, room or apartment

Depending on your general hygiene and upkeep of your living quarters this activity could mean a lot or very little. As above, so below. The living quarters or area where you work is a small reflection of your inner state of mind. Changing a dirty, disorganized area into one of order is not only a way to energize and calm your mind (aka banish unwanted elements) but also a good way to put other elements of your life in order.

Russian coldwater dousing

During my study of the Russian martial art Systema I came across the practice of cold water dowsing. The practitioners of systema claimed that dowsing (i.e. dumping a bucket of cold water over your head and body) twice a day had many health benefits. I practiced the dowsing once or twice a day for almost a year straight. It was possibly one of the hardest things I have ever done on a daily basis. Each and every time I found myself in the backyard or tub with a bucket of cold water about to go over my head I was as hesitant as the first time to dump it over myself. While I cannot make any claims as to the health benefits of the cold water dowsing I can tell you that for me it was very energizing. The rush from the cold water woke my body up in a way that can only be experienced and I was always much more alert afterwards. In retrospect I felt the dowsing made me more alert during the 8-9 months I did it consistently. Be it the placebo effect, the feeling of doing something that your body 100% rejects the idea of, or something much deeper it seemed to have a profound ability to change my state of mind.

Take a look at Vladamir Vasiliev's book on Russian Systema. It is radically different that most martial arts and cold water dowsing is one of many strange elements in that system of martial arts.

Doing something stupid/incredibly childish
If you are reading this book I am sure you are aware of many ways to do this. This can be done alone or in public (which is much braver and packs more heat generally). One example which requires a partner and is a 100% guarantee to change your state to one of laughter is the following. It is powerful when done with the right person and possibly even reading about it will work. It is:

The Snack Game

This can be done solo or with two or more people. One person begins by saying the name of a snack or desert in a death metal/growling voice. Imagine the Cookie Monster saying "Cookies" for example. The other person or people in the group then have to keep the game going by coming up with new snacks and then take turns stating them one at a time in the same deep growly voice. Increased accent can be given to the voice and the food items used can be limitless. While this might sound incredibly stupid (Because it truly is) with the right person/group you may end up tears. Right this moment as you read this say "Cupcakes" in the growly voice and see.

Voluntary Silence

Being quiet is an act so simple, yet so hard to do. While it is unlikely anyone reading this book is willing to take a vow of silence on the level of a monk even a few hours can be mind changing. Words are the most basic tools involved in life or magic (i.e. brain change willed) and shutting down your stream of generally freely flowing verbiage is one way to control the self. Buckminster Fuller, one of the most influential American thinkers and writer of the twentieth century refused to talk for over a year as a form of meditation and way to study words as tools.

6. Wolverine Walking/Contrarian Walking.

Wolverines in the wild will pick a direction of travel and go regardless of what obstacles stand before them. The human example would be to pick a direction and within your limits go in as straight of a line as possible by walking through over and around whatever is in your way.

Contrarian walking simply involves not walking where people are supposed to or have been conditioned to walk. Not using sidewalks, pathways even if just a few feet off the beaten path. Walking like this for certain time or extended period must be experienced for its value to be best understood.

Power Posing

This method is easy and according to Harvard Professor Amy Cuddy can prepare you for intense social situations by increasing your testosterone and lowering your cortisol levels (stress). Power posing involves standing in specific poses for approximately 2 minutes. These are dominate poses and include standing with your hands in the air as if you have just won something and standing with your hands on your hips like a super hero. A simple online search of "Amy Cuddy Power Posing" will put you in touch with a very detailed description/video of this method.

Appendix 2: CHIR creation notes and other handwritten draft examples

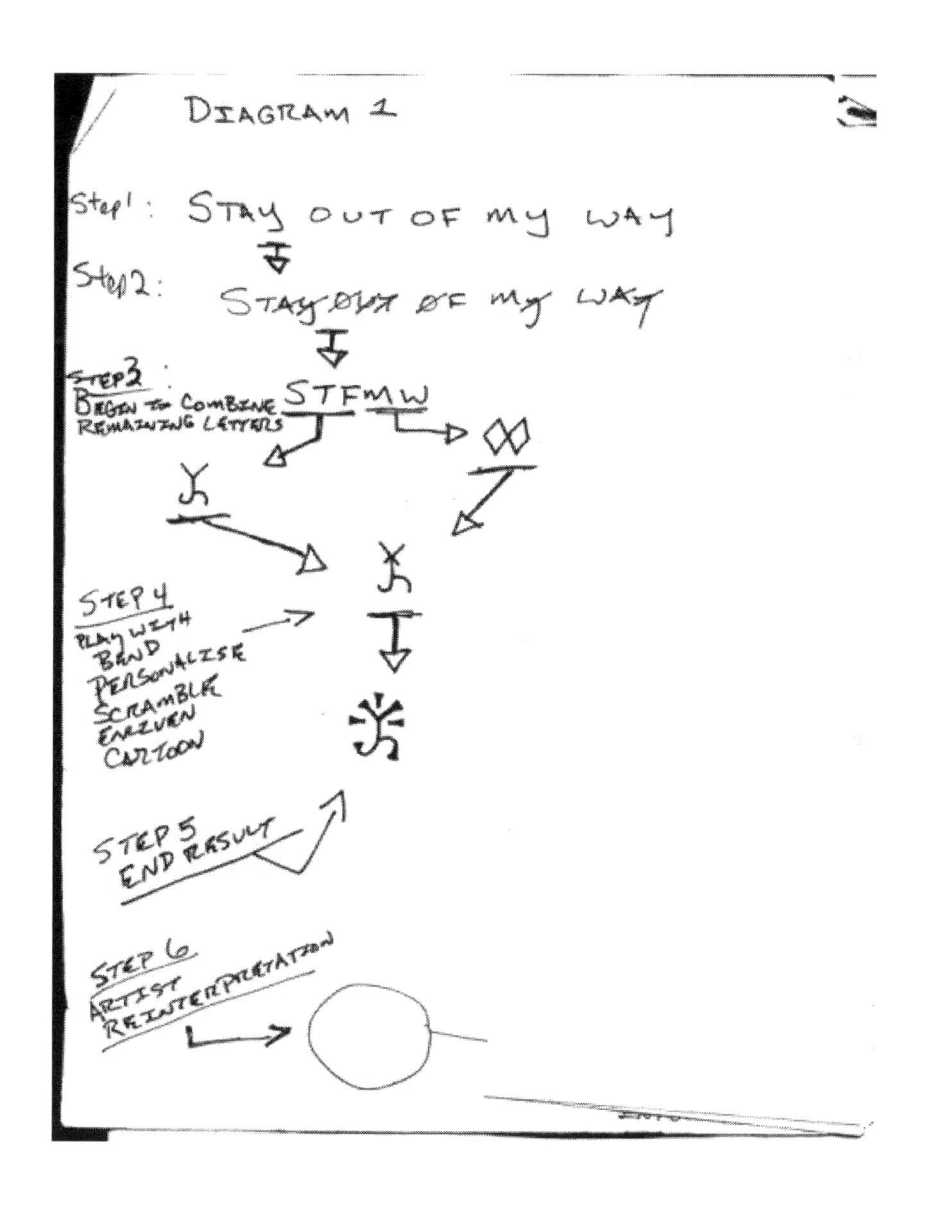

CHAPEL OF THE INFINITE READER

ChoIR — • INTENT IS TO CREAT A SIGIL
• THAT ENCAPSULATES THE MINDSPACE OF INTENSE STUDY/READING AND THE ENJOYMENT AND FEELINGS THAT GO ALONG WITH IT.

STEP 1

8 NAMES OF MOST INFLUENTIAL AUTHORS, MINDS.

1. JOSEPH CAMPBELL
2. J. KRISHNAMURTI
3. RAM DASS
4. ALAN WATTS
5. ALEISTER CROWLEY
6. CHARLES BUKOWSKI
7. TERENCE McKENNA
8. ROY EUGENE DAVIS

STEP 2 — ASSIGN NAMES TO THE WHEEL

STEP 3 — CREATE AN INDIVIDUAL SIGIL FOR EACH NAME ON THE WHEEL. IN THIS CASE USING THE REMOVAL OF ALL VOWELS AND DOUBLE LETTERS.

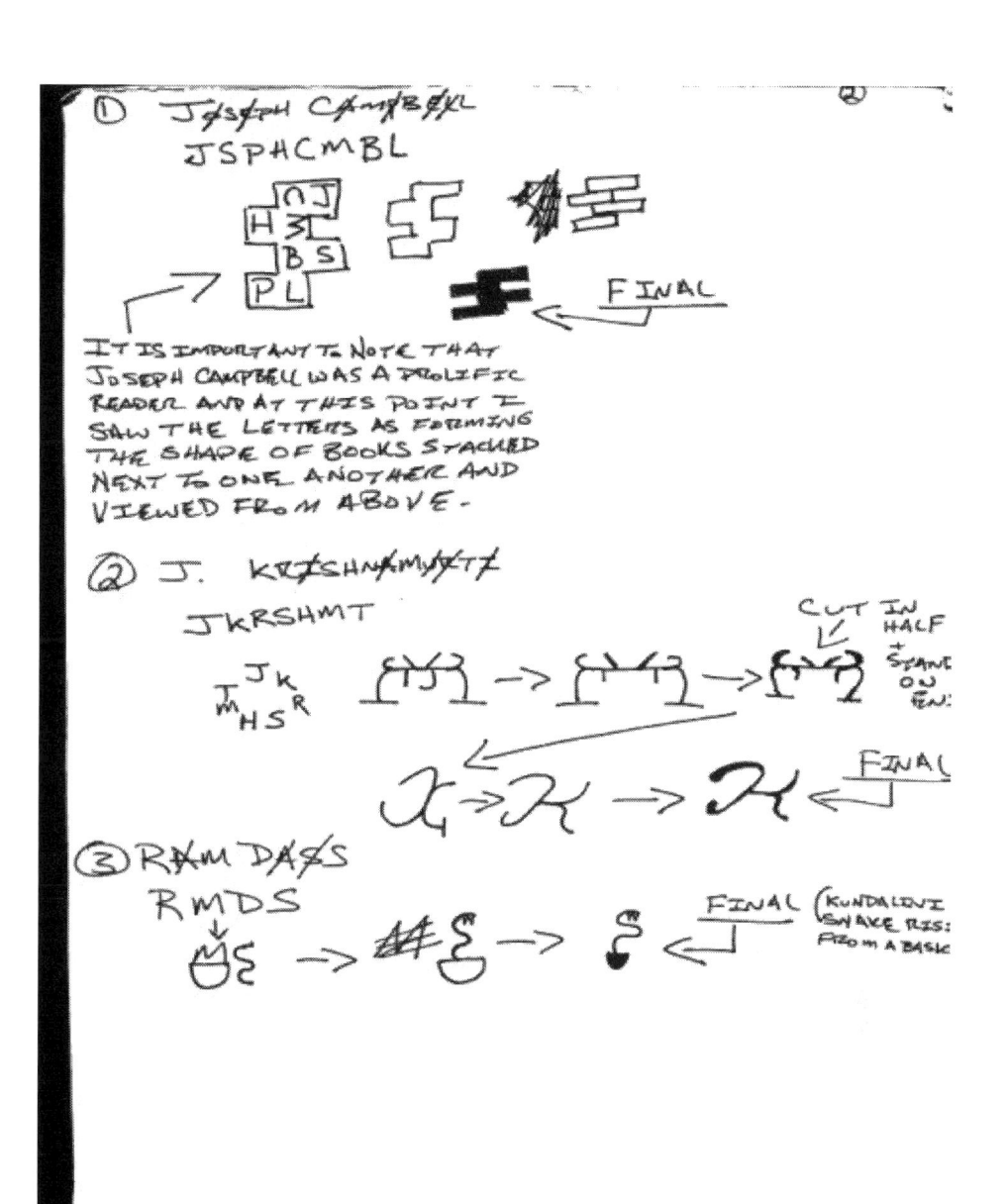

① J~~oseph~~ C~~a~~mpb~~e~~ll
JSPHCMBL

[diagrams]

→ FINAL

IT IS IMPORTANT TO NOTE THAT
JOSEPH CAMPBELL WAS A PROLIFIC
READER AND AT THIS POINT I
SAW THE LETTERS AS FORMING
THE SHAPE OF BOOKS STACKED
NEXT TO ONE ANOTHER AND
VIEWED FROM ABOVE.

② J. KR~~I~~SHN~~A~~M~~U~~RT~~I~~
JKRSHMT

[diagrams] CUT IN HALF + STAND ON END:

[diagrams] ← FINAL

③ R~~a~~m D~~a~~s~~s~~
RMDS

[diagrams] → [diagrams] → [diagrams] ← FINAL (KUNDALINI SNAKE RIS: FROM A BASK)

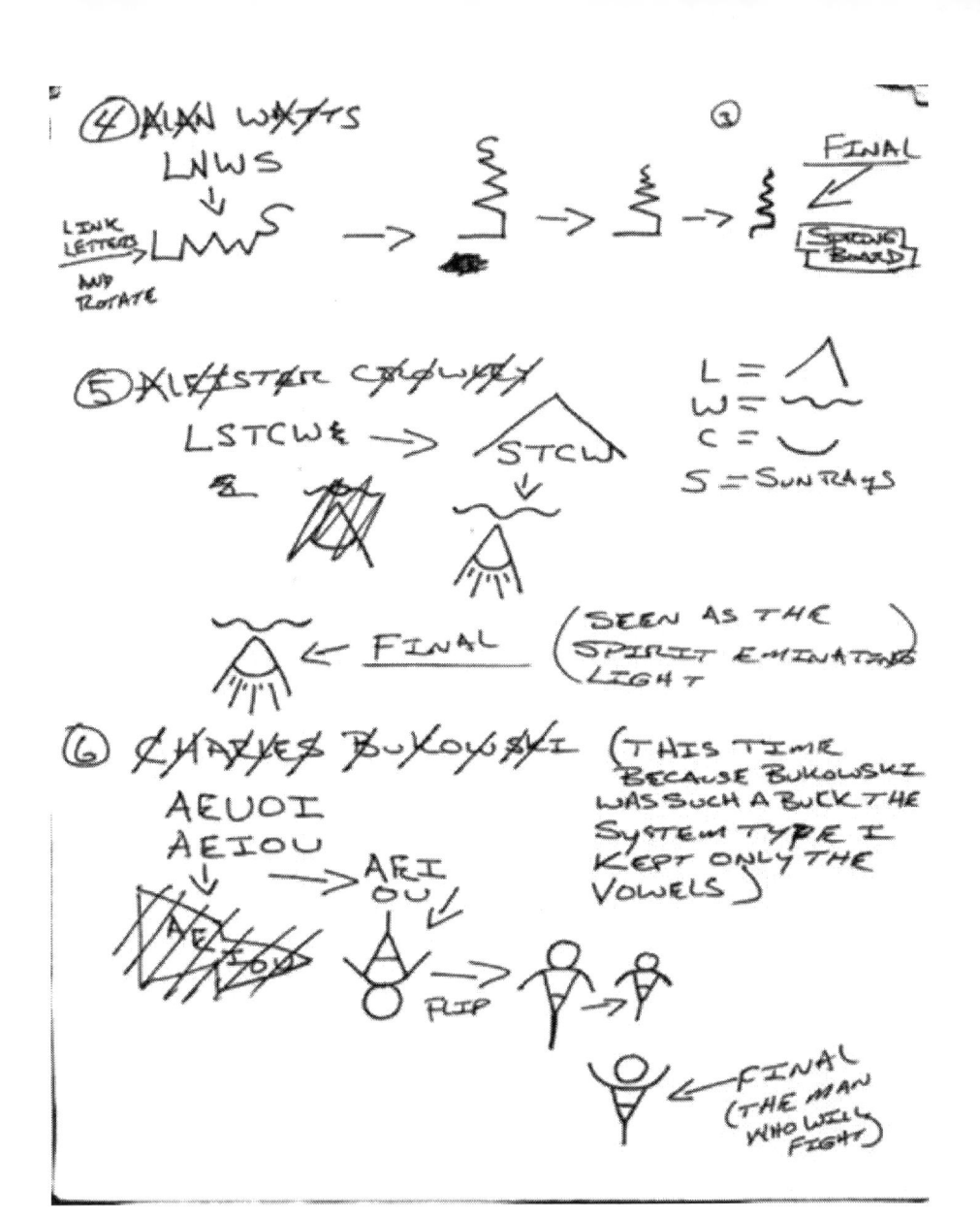

④ ALAN WATTS
   LNWS
   ↓
LINK LETTERS → LMWS ~ → L⌃ → L⌃ → L⌃   FINAL ⚡
AND   [SPRING BOARD]
ROTATE

⑤ ALEISTER CROWLEY   L = ⋀
   LSTCW & → /STCW\   W = ~
   & ✗   C = ∪
                           S = SUN RAYS

   ⛰☀ ← FINAL   (SEEN AS THE SPIRIT EMINATING LIGHT)

⑥ CHARLES BUKOWSKI   (THIS TIME BECAUSE BUKOWSKI WAS SUCH A BUCK THE SYSTEM TYPE I KEPT ONLY THE VOWELS)
   AEUOI
   AEIOU
   ↓   → ARI
          OU ✓
   ✗   → 🙂 → 🧍 → 🧍
            FLIP

            🙌 ← FINAL (THE MAN WHO WILL FIGHT)

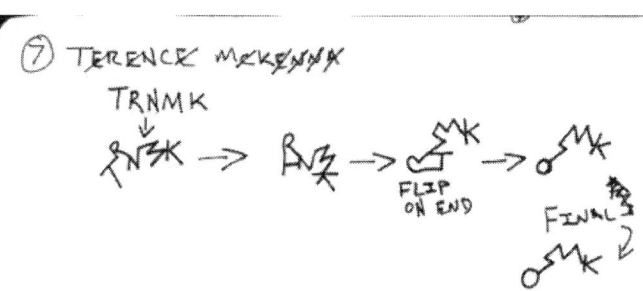

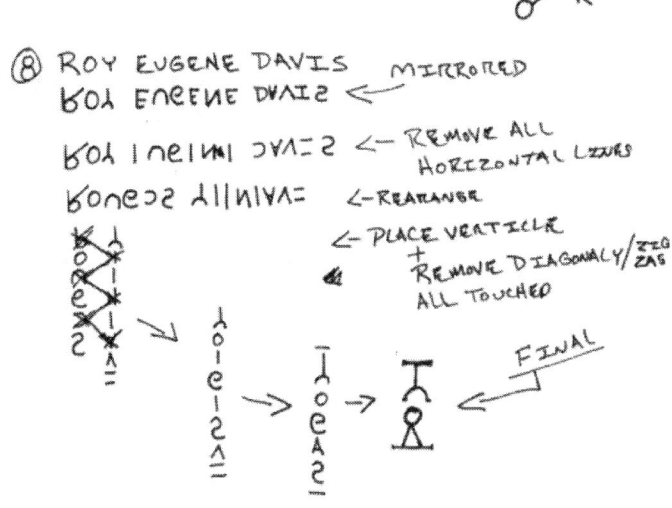

⑦ TERENCE McKENNA
   TRNMK

[diagram: TRNMK → BNMK → flipped form (FLIP ON END) → circle-MK form → FINAL circle-MK form]

⑧ ROY EUGENE DAVIS ← MIRRORED
   ROY EUGENE DAVIS ←
   ROY IИEIИI ƆVΛIƧ ← REMOVE ALL HORIZONTAL LINES
   ROYEƆƧ ΛIIИIVΛ= ← REARRANGE
                    ← PLACE VERTICLE
                    +
                    REMOVE DIAGONALY/ ZIG ZAG
                    ALL TOUCHED

[diagram progression → Toei2As → FINAL figure]

HAND DRAFTS OF FINAL SET COMBINED

Appendix 3: Origami/Masu Box Instructions

This is a very basic origami masu box that with practice can be folded more and more geometrical with every try.

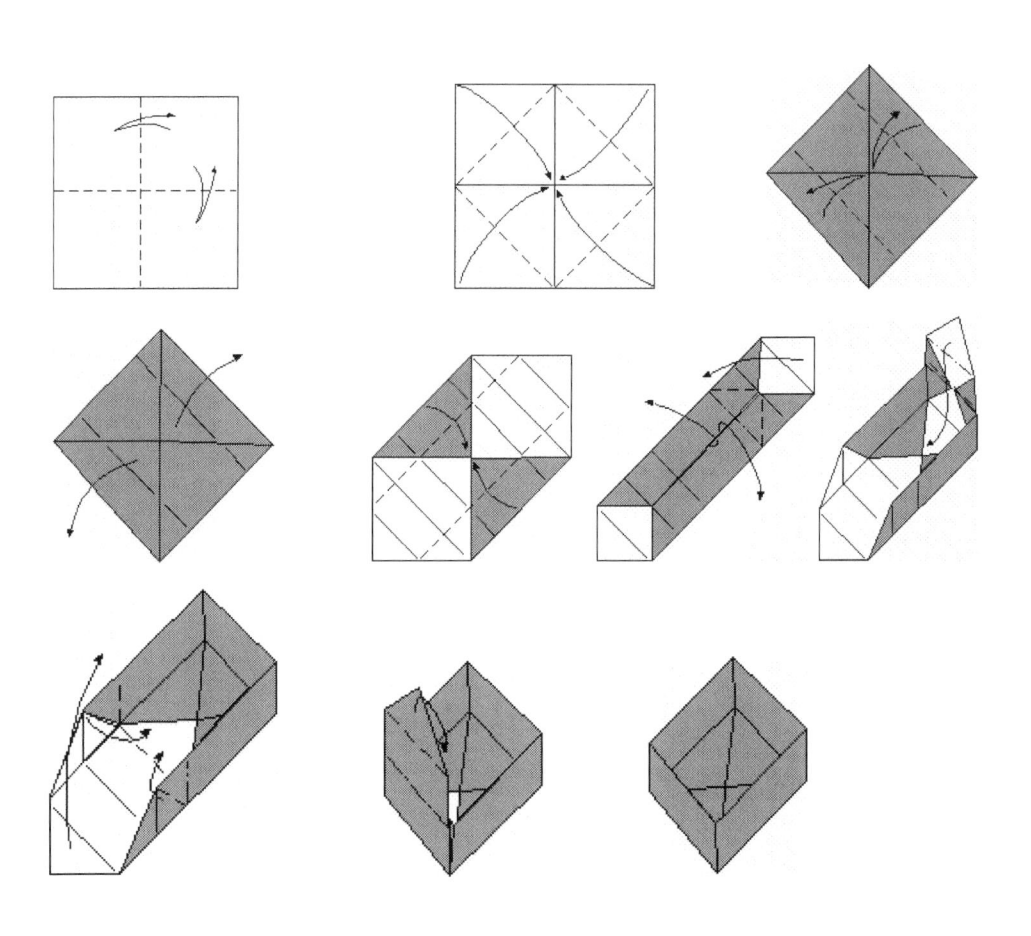

Special thanks to:

Brian Locher, Joshua Clayton, W.K. Luce & J. Luce, Worthington P. Loaf, Musashi of MMA.TV, E&I Geer, Eric Vernor, D. Junk, J. Baird for being understanding while not understanding, The 3 of clubs, KEOP72, K. Wetoskey and the Kriya yoga group, Razz & Jamie, Frozen peas, Gordon Hester, Hyde Brothers Books and their amazing occult section, The creators of the Principia Discordia, The threshold guardians of 2010, Freddy Ray and the Gypsy Vault tattoo parlor.

Endnotes

1. Even by early Christians disguised the cross in swastika like symbols and the cross according to Rudolph Koch in his work *The Book of Signs*.
2. For more information on this concept read .O. Spares *The Book of Pleasure*, and his other works.
3. Head of the Mande Muda system of Penjak Silat, a martial art which included what Suwanda called *Silat Magic*. He died in 2000 but his system is carried on by his siblings.
4. Point in life or moment of extreme worry. "This system of sigils is believed by taking it up as a hobby at a time of great disappointment or sorrow" A.O. Sparre, *The Book of Pleasure*
5. The Disinfo lecture given by Grant Morrison on *Magic and the use of Sigils* is recommended.
6. Alan Watts with a gift for the westernization of eastern philosophy and Buddhism once stated "Once you get the message, hang up the phone."
7. A large number of Terence McKenna's lectures are available on the *Psychedelic Salon* podcast (Free on Itunes). Many other excellent lectures by speakers are also available thanks to the effort of Lorenzo Hagerty and are highly recommended

Illustrations

Pointillism illustrations by artist Freddy Ray of the Gypsy Vault.

Hand drawn ink illustrations and sigils by author unless otherwise noted.

Recommended Reading/Bibliography

What follows are only a few of the recommendations which the author deems very relevant to the subject of this book and is no way intended to be an exhaustive list. This list represents a compilation of material which the author has found informative and highly recommends.

Occult and Psyhcology

The Book of Pleasure by Austin Osman Spare

Man, Myth & Magic, an Illustrated Encyclopedia of the Supernatural. Edited by Richard Cavendish.

The Black Arts by Richard Cavendish

Book 4 by Aleister Crowley

The Book of Law, Aleister Crowley

Undoing Yourself with Energized Mediation by Christopher Hyatt

Prometheus Rising by Robert Anton Wilson

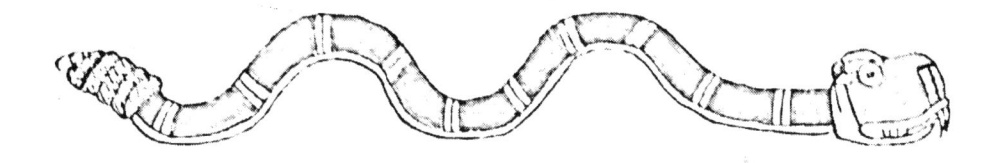

Liber Null & Psychonaut by Peter J Carroll

The Great Beast by Colin Wilson

Magic, The Western Tradition by Francis King

The Weiser Concise Guide to Aleister Crowley. Richard Kaczynski, Ph.D.

Portable Darkness: An Aleister Crowley Reader by Edited by Scott Michaelson

The Book of Lies, The Disinformation Guide to Magick and the Occult. Edited by Richard Metzger.

Hoodoo Mysteries, Folk Magic, Mysticism & Rituals by Ray Malbrough.

Principia Discordia by Malaclypse the Younger & Lord Ravenhurst

Discordia, Hail Eris Goddess of All Chaos and Confusion by Malaclypse the Younger and Omar Ravenhurst.

Journey to Ixtlan, The Lessons of Don Juan by Carlos Castaneda

The Book of the Subgenious by The Subgenious Foundation

Giordano Bruno and Renaissance Science by Hilary Gatti

Eastern Philosophy/Technique

The Book by Alan Watts

Be Here Now by Ram Dass

The Only Dance There is by Ram Dass

Tao Te Ching by Lao Tzu

Awaken Healing Energy Through the Tao by Mantak Chia

Hagakure by Yamamoto Tsunetomo

Autobiography of a Yogi by Pramahansa Yogananda

Various Topics

The Book of Signs by Rudolf Koch

Sense Relaxation, Below the Mind by Bernard Gunther

The Great Origami Book by Zulal Ayture-Scheele

Illustrations

Pointillism illustrations are courtesy of author collection, created by Freddy Ray. Hand drawn illustrations and photography are by author unless otherwise noted.

ABOUT THE AUTHOR

Vincent K. Luce first began his explorations into the occult after his mother helped him apply for a library card and subsequently paid no attention at all to what books he ended up taking home. Largely in response to the so-called "Satanic Panic" in the 1980s, Luce developed a strange fascination with lost, forbidden, or otherworldly knowledge. He started out with the simple but perverse intention to scare the shit out of himself, but serendipitously came away with unique insight into what the elements of magic reveal about the human mind.

After receiving a degree in criminal justice from Indiana University, Luce began a career in law enforcement. He continued his research into the occult alongside his professional duties, but over time his view of the topic shifted from a focus on how frightening it could be to how he might apply some of the underlying psychological principles to his work, and to his life beyond it. But, aside from deciphering a few Dutch hex signs that had his fellow officers baffled and pointing out to a special agent that he was completely misinterpreting a poster on a kiosk in a mall, which turned out to be the cover of *The Necronomicon*, Luce had few chances to put his ever-growing knowledge to use on the job.

After twenty years of study, he wanted to get deeper into the practices he'd read so much about. So, over the past several years, Luce has been working with rituals from various systems of magic in an attempt to understand their impact on the practitioner's mind. In addition to pursuing further research into fields like chaos and sigil magic, he has read widely on psychology and comparative mythology. In experimenting with a variety of occult practices, Luce has arrived at the central insight that what magic boils down to is knowledge of the self and the will to change one's own mind.

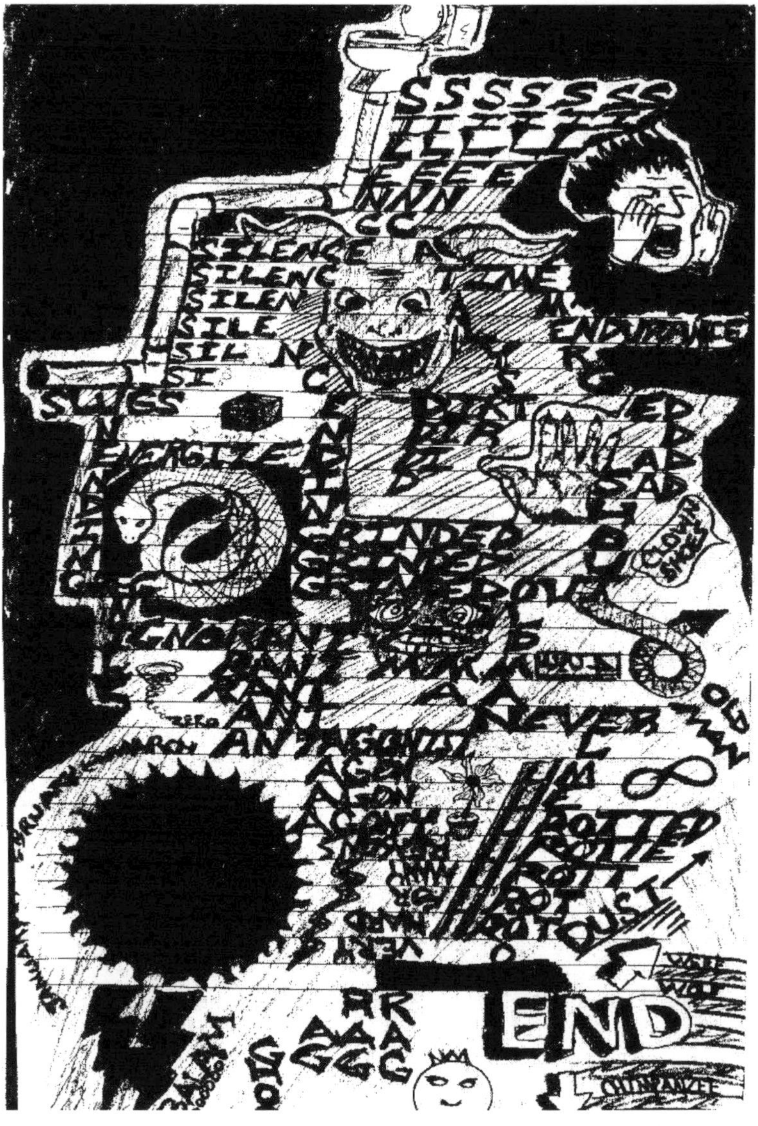
SSSSSS
SILENCE
SILENC
SILEN
SILE
SIL
SI
ENDURANCE
SLUGS
ENERGIZE
GRINDED
CLOWN SHOES
IGNORANT
NEVER
ANTAGONIST
OLD MAN
ROTTED
END
CHIMPANZEE

Film Noir

My Shadow Bride

Jimmy Vargas

"She was stationed at the crossroads of the last breath of my past life and the first of this gimcrack one...I call her My Shadow Bride"

A phantasmagorical tale of a Los Angeles crooner racketeer Jimmy Vargas and his affair with a Sorceress from the San Francisco Mission Liliana Scarlatta, who is the avatar of Hollywood Queens of the nineteen forties, Hayworth, Ava Gardner, and the infamous Black Dahlia.

300 pages

$24.99 USD

May 2013 RELEASE

Temple of Lily

Jimmy Vargas

"Around twilight I stalk the Dreamland taxi dance palace, torching the cracked keys of a Steinway 88's, trying in vain to raise your scarlet veil, Lily, with our tune "The Girl you Left Behind."

Part two of the phantasmagorical tale of a Los Angeles crooner racketeer Jimmy Vargas.

300 pages

$24.99 USD

October 2013 RELEASE

Paranormal

Most Haunted: Scariest Places on Earth

Corvis Nocturnum

Join occult researcher and author Corvis Nocturnum, as he guides you through some of the most bizarre and creepy places on the face of the planet. Many have long been rumored to be haunted and all of them are chilling to see! Photographs and facts on places such as the Boney Church, Danvers State Mental Hospital which was the filming location and inspiration for the horror movie Session 9, Alcatraz, the skull lined catacombs under Paris and much more!

ISBN-13: 978-1470015480

148 pages

$16.95 USD

Paranormal Investigation Basics

Mark Davis

Mark Davis breaks through the mystiscm of paranormal investigation, simply and fully detailing the skills and equipment needed for anyone interested in exploring the spirit world. *Paranormal Investigations: The Basics* give a details history and terms of the field and offers a wealth of knowledge for this fascinating and popular field.

Mark Davis is the Co-host of *The Shadows Radio*

ISBN-13: 978-1475006087

$19.95 USD

200 pages

Occult/New Age

Promethean Flame

Corvis Nocturnum

Exploring the lineage of those who challenged dogmatic thinking, from the Renaissance and our modern day, *Promethean Flame* delves deep into religion, philosophy and the arts to explain the importance that the challengers of the past still have on our future. Covering everything from the earliest secret societies such as the Templars and Chaos magicians to Rosicrucian Society, The Masonic Order, and facts on fascinating key individuals such as Leonardo Da Vinci, Napoleon Bonaparte, The Hellfire Club all the way up to The Golden Dawn occultists. Corvis links the works of scientists and creative thinkers like Aristotle, Plato, and Socrates to the cause. As well the lives and works of a multitude of Decadent Romantics such as Mary and Percy Shelly, Poe, and Lord Byron are examined.

ISBN-13: 978-0615242576   232 page, $19.95 USD

Necromancy the forbidden art

Lucien Rofocale

Discover the history of Demons and their magical sigils, how to work with them and those who have in the past.

ISBN-13: 978-1460972649

116 pages

$9.95 USD

Collected Works of Eliphas Levi
Dark Moon Press

Collected is the written works of Eliphas Levi, containing in one volume *The Key of Mysteries and Dogma* and *Dogma et Ritual de la Haute Magie*, volumes one and two, all in one manual. Translations by Arthur E. Waite

600 pages
$29.99 USD

Aleister Crowley: Selected works of the Beast
Dark Moon Press

The infamous 'Beast' as the occultist was called is now collected in one volume. Works such as *LIBER 777, Book of the Black Serpent,* and *MAGICK WITHOUT TEARS*.

ISBN-13: 978-1467983563
600 pages
$29.99 USD

The Psychic Vampire s Guide to subtle Body Language & Psionics

Lono F. Vespertillio

The powerful inter-connections of the body mundras as well as energy patterns we all have are easily explained and offer the reader basic and advanced techniques to alter our reality. Body language and how to work with others to manipulate situations from magic, to business to the bedroom.

ISBN-13: 978-1460970201

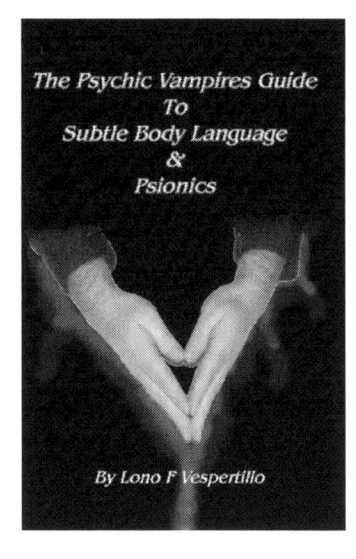

240 pages

$19.95 USD

Walking the Path of the Ancient Ways a collection of magic by various pagan authors

Corvis Nocturnum

Pagan authors from various backgrounds share their story on being pagan in the modern world. Insightful and thought provoking. With writings by Starr Morgayne, Corvis Nocturnum, Andrieh Vitimus and many more known and new voices.

ISBN-13: 978-1470034641

Pages: 200

$19.99 USD

Bewitching Beauty: Bringing out your inner Goddess, naturally
Starr Morgayne

Women of all ages are concerned about their skin, their bodies and growing older. In this book the author offers simple yet effective, personally tested recipes based on readily available ingredients, and her own unique perspective to help get you in touch with Mother Nature and yourself. Regardless of what stage of life you are in this book can be a positive addition to your journey.

ISBN-13: 978-1451585872
200 pages
$16.95 USD

MAGICKAL MANNERS: A Guide to Magickal Etiquette
Puck Shadowdrake

"An extensive overview of the practices and etiquette of the entire Neo Pagan community. An excellent resource for chaplains as well as for students seeking a spiritual path." Kerr Cuhulain, author of *Pagan Religions: A Handbook for Diversity Training*

ISBN-13: 978-1481910958

Pages: 600
Price: $39.99 USD
Spring 2013

JOURNEYS FROM THE MEADOW: A Book of Guided Mediations
Puck Shadowdrake

Puck Shadowdrake, the author of *MAGICKAL MANNERS: A Guide to Magickal Etiquette* brings you his collection of meditations to guide the modern witch through their various journeys through the path for relaxation, healing the body and contacting your deities, spirit guides and much more.

Pages: TBA

Price: $19.99 USD

Spring 2014

The Vampire Ritual Book
Michelle Belanger

The Vampire Ritual Book was originally commissioned for use within the *Sanguinarium*. Although many of the seasonal rites later appeared as calendar dates in the *Vampyre Almanac*, the rituals themselves were never widely distributed. In 2003, a limited-edition was prepared for print, but these rare books were circulated only to a very few. This book is a reprint of the 2003 limited edition.

ISBN-13: 978-1442118089

160 pages

$16.95 USD

The Devil/Demonology

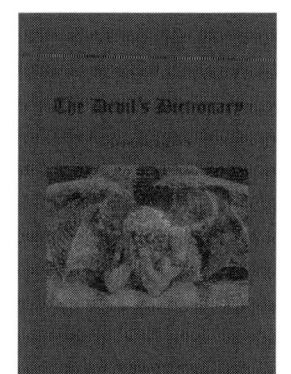

The Devil's Dictionary by Ambrose Bierce
Dark Moon Press

The Devil's Dictionary is a satirical reference book written by Ambrose Bierce. The book offers re-interpretations of terms in the English language, lampooning cant and political doublespeak. It was originally published in 1906 as *The Cynic's Word Book* before being retitled in 1911.

ISBN-13: 978-1460970003

208 pages
$16.95 USD

Sympathy for the Devil; A Collection of Sinister Tales
Dark Moon Press

A series of short stories following the exploits of "Old Nick" through ancient days to our modern day. A must have collection of classics.

ISBN-13: 978-1460969960
404 pages
$29.95 USD

D is for Demon
Michelle Belanger

A devilishly fun romp through the alphabet in the tradition of Edward Gorey. Inspired by Michelle Belanger's *Dictionary of Demons* and illustrated by artist Jackie Williams. Madcap, witty, and irreverent at times, this is a picture book for adults and not children.
ISBN-13: 978-1456447922
76 pages
$9.95 USD

Sympathy for the Devil; A Collection of Sinister Tales
Corvis Nocturnum, Beelzebub

A collection of humorous and scathing thoughts by history's greatest writers, comedians and thinkers. From as far back as Niccolò Machiavelli, to Ann Rand and Anton LaVey, it also has the sharp wit of Mark Twain, George Carlin and many others who have been the Devil's Advocates on Earth. Compiled by Corvis Nocturnum and commentary by Ol' Scratch on his reflections of his champions, it will make you both ponder and laugh at various aspects of the human condition.
180 pages
$17.99 USD
Spring 2013

Sumerian Exorcism: Mahick, Demons, and the Lost Art of Marduk

Michelle Belanger

Demonic possession, wicked spells, and ancient bindings all come together in this exploration of Sumerian magick and exorcism. Discover the roots of modern demonology and explore prayers and incantations from the very cradle of Western civilization. This book focuses on the original writings themselves, so you can read for yourself spells drawn from the Maklu Texts and other Sumerian magickal tablets. The translations present a fascinating view of Sumero-Babylonian religion, myth, and demonology. The gods Shamash, Marduk, and Ea play pivotal roles in the fight against the dark powers of Lilitum, Labartu, and the Utukku - a host of evil spirits dedicated to sowing destruction and disease amongst humanity.

ISBN-13: 978-1482521733

180 pages

$17.99 USD

The Truth About Demons

Raven Bloodstone

The Truth About Demons is not another book attempting to classify or identify demons. This book is the author's own experiences, not based on religious documentation.

ISBN-13: 978-1479324477

200 pages

$19.95 USD

Satan's Minion's: A Guide to Fallen Angel's, Demons and other Dark Creatures

Corvis Nocturnum

Join occult researcher and author Corvis Nocturnum in the quest to uncover everything from the story and evolution of the mother of all dark creatures, Lilith to the Fallen Angels and many mythic creatures. Featuring artwork by the author, as well as fantasy artist Joseph Vargo and other classic artists.

ISBN-13: 978-1466484962

186 pages

$16.95 USD

Goetic Demons: New theories on Demonic Magick

Lucien Rofocale

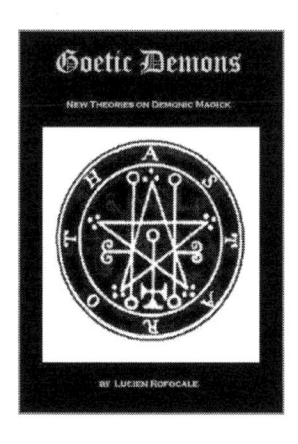

Get a glimpse into the ancient and forbidden art of necromancy and explore aspects of this Black Art history and practice of summoning spirits for spiritual protection to wisdom. Learn the tools and rituals needed in this fascinating work.

ISBN-13: 978-1466335295

100 pages

$9.95 USD

Zombies

BRAAAAAAAAINS a zombie anthology
Dark Moon Press

Dark Moon Press brings you a collection of zombie short stories by various new authors.

ISBN-13: 978-1475296983
$19.99 USD

BRAAAAAAAAINS II a zombie anthology
Dark Moon Press

Dark Moon Press brings you a collection of zombie short stories by various new authors.

$19.99 USD

FALL 2013

Vampires

Allure of the Vampire: Our Sexual Attraction to the Undead

Corvis Nocturnum

The mere mention of vampires used to be enough to make people think of a nocturnal predator. But over the centuries the vampire has changed from monstrous villain to sexual object, for both men and women alike. Allure of the Vampire examines our intimate attraction to these beings in a detailed manner. Now, join occult author Corvis Nocturnum as he reveals the fascinating evolution of this icon as it has lured and enticed us in folklore, film and books from the days of ancient civilization to the living breathing inhabitants of our modern subculture, the vampire community.

ISBN-13: 978-1448658947

284 pages

$19.99 USD

Sacred Hunger

Michelle Belanger

Author Michelle Belanger has fascinated and informed readers about the vampire in folklore, fiction, and fact since the early 90s. Find out why author Bram Stoker wrote about vampires -- and what real-life psychic vampire inspired the figure of Dracula. Learn about the history and development of the modern community of real vampires. Explore the allure of the vampire in modern culture, and meet members of the vampire underground who have made this potent archetype a fundamental part of their lives

ISBN-13: 978-1411654211

142 pages

$16.95 USD

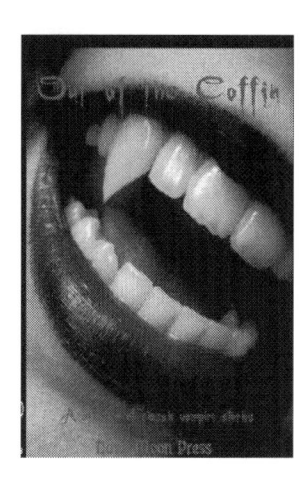

Out of the Coffin; A Collection of Classic Vampire Stories
Dark Moon Press

A collection of classic vampire stories such as *Carmella, The Vampire* by Rudyard Kipling, and other tales from our past. A treasure trove of stalkers in the night!

ISBN-13: 978-1460969939
380 pages
$29.95 USD

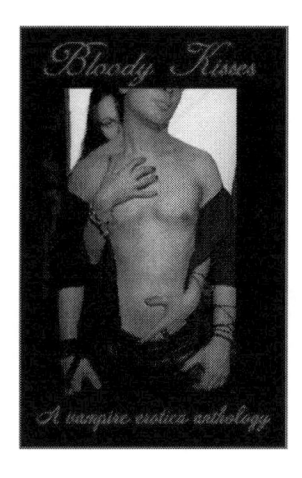

Bloody Kisses a vampire erotica anthology
Dark Moon Press
A hot and steamy collection of blood soaked tales from authors such as Michelle Belanger, Raven Digitalis, Corvis Nocturnum, Mora Zoranokov and more!
WARNING: Adult Content

ISBN-13: 9781257291663
192 pages
$17.95 USD

Bloody Kisses II a vampire erotica anthology

Dark Moon Press

A hot and steamy collection of blood soaked tales from many new authors!

WARNING: Adult Content

192 pages

$19.99 USD

FALL 2013

La Morte Amore: Vampire Poetry of the 1800s

Dark Moon Press

Der Vampire by Heinrich August Eckenfelder (1748)
Lenore by Gottfied August Bürger (1773)
Die Braut von Korinth by Johann Wolfgang von Goethe (1797)
Christabel by Samuel Taylor Coleridge (date unknown)
Thalaba the Destroyer by Robert Southey (1800)
The Giaour by Lord Byron (1813)
La Belle Dame Sans Merci by John Keats (1819)
Lamia by John Keats (1820)
The Vampire Bride by Henry Liddell (1833)
La Morte Amoureuse by Theophile Gautier (1836)
The Vampyre by James Clerk Maxwell (1845)
Le Vampire by Charles Baudelaire (1857)
Les Metamorphoses du Vampire by Charles Baudelaire (date unknown)
The Vampire by Rudyard Kipling (189
7)*The Vampire* by Jacques LeClercq

ISBN-13: 978-1478381174

122 pages

$9.99 USD

Crimson Tales A vampire anthology
Dark Moon Press

Dark Moon Press brings you a collection of vampire fiction from variety of talented new authors.

ISBN-13: 978-1479140466

$19.95 USD

298 pages

Immortal
Michelle Belanger

A mysterious couple, a vampire tour, and a Gothic rock band all converge on the tourist trap of modern Transylvania, where an archaeological crew seeks to uncover the real resting place of Vlad Tepes -- the man known to the world as Dracula. When real vampires are unleashed upon the unsuspecting tourists, one woman must reveal an age-old secret or risk the lives of everyone around her.

ISBN-13: 9781257718108

204 pages

$16.96 USD

Classic Horror

Edgar Alan Poe: 200 Years of the Macabre

Dark Moon Press

Edgar Allan Poe 200 years of the macabre A complete collection of his short stories and poetry from the most recognized master of the macabre.

ISBN-13: 978-1460970058

224 pages

$19.95 USD

Chilling Tales of H.P. Lovecraft

Dark Moon Press

Dark Moon Press brings you a collection of works from the master of horror. Stories such as: *The Alchemist, The Beast in the Cave, Beyond the Wall of Sleep, The Case of Charles Dexter Ward, The Cats of Ulthare, The Descendant.*

ISBN-13: 978-1466342811

282 pages

$29.99 USD

Chilling Tales of H.P. Lovecraft II
Dark Moon Press

Dark Moon Press brings you a collection of works from the master of horror. Stories included are: *Dreams in the Witch House, The Dunwich Horror, The Evil Clergyman, The Festival, The Hunter of the Dark, Herbert West: Reanimator, In the Vault.*

ISBN-13: 978-1466345706

310 pages

$29.99 USD

Chilling Tales of H. P. Lovecraft III

Dark Moon Press brings you the third book in the collection of this master of horror. H.P. Lovecraft inspired countless writers and artists.

This third volume contains:
The Call of Cthulhu
Celephais
The Doom That Came to Sarnath
The Lurking Fear
Nyarlathotep
The Nameless City
The Other Gods
The Unnamable
Azathoth
The Moon-Bog
The Thing on the Doorstep
The Shadow Out of Time

ISBN-13: 978-1478373841
368 pages
$29.99 USD

Gothic Classic Horror

Dark Moon Press

Dark Moon Press brings you a collection of the best horror classics with stories like:

The Legend of Sleepy Hollow by Washington Irving
The Fall of the House of Usher Edgar Allan Poe
Dracula's Guest Bram Stoker
The Dunwick Horror H.P. Lovecraft
The Canterville Ghost Oscar Wilde

ISBN-13: 978-1479129379

$19.99

260 pages

Gothic Classic Horror II

Dark Moon Press

Dark Moon Press brings you a collection of the best horror classics with stories like:

The Castle of Otranto Horace Walpole
Dr. Jekyll and Mr. Hyde Robert Luis Stevenson
The Vampyre John William Polidori
The The Masque of the Red Death Edgar Allan Poe

$19.99

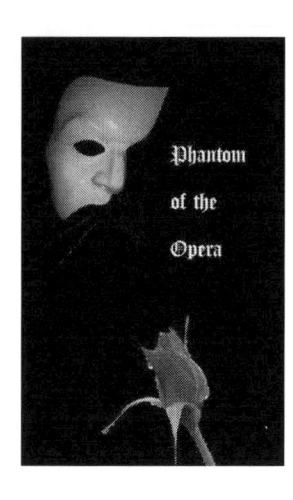

Phanthom of the Opera
Dark Moon Press

Dark Moon Press brings you the classic Phantom of the Opera. This novel by French writer Gaston Leroux. It was first published as a serialisation inLe Gaulois from September 23, 1909 .

$19.99
FALL 2013

Dracula
Bram Stoker
Dark Moon Press

Dark Moon Press brings the original Dracula, complete with illustration from the first printing interior as the cover art.

$19.99
FALL 2015

Dante's Inferno Purgatorio and Paradisio

Dark Moon Press

Dark Moon Press brings you a collection of Italian masterpiece of classics of the entire saga. The allegory telling of the journey of Dante's through what is largely the medieval concept of Hell, guided by the Roman poet Virgil. In the poem, Hell is depicted as nine circles of suffering located within the Earth

$19.99

FALL 2013

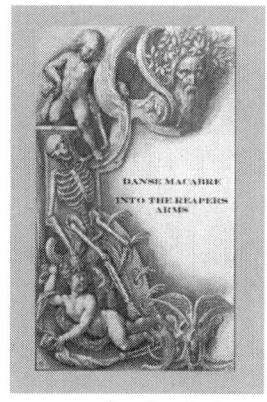

Danse Macabre: Into the Reaper's Arms

Dark Moon Press

Inspired by old European historical references to art and literature on Death during the Middle Ages and on through the Renaissance period this book shows the breathtaking beauty in the rich artworks of the time. *Dance Macabre: Into the Reaper's Arms* has classic poetry from Charles Baudelaire, Robert Louis Stevenson, Emily Dickson, Lord Byron and a dozen other masters of melancholy.

ISBN-13: 978-1460969816

120 pages

$16.95 USD

General Horror/miscellaneous

Spectral Hauntings Anthology of the Supernatural
Dark Moon Press

Dark Moon Press brings you a collection of ghost and paranormal short stories by various new authors.

ISBN-13: 978-1477649053
300 pages
$19.95 USD

Claw and Fang Tooth and Nail a werecreature anthology
Dark Moon Press

Dark Moon Press brings you a collection of Were creature short stories by various new authors.

ISBN-13: 978-1477639092
248 pages
$19.95 USD

These Haunted Dreams

Michelle Belanger

Dark, sensuous, and lyrical, the supernatural fiction of author Michelle Belanger has enchanted the readers of Shadowdance, Necropolis, and Wicked Mysticsince 1991. Now, collected for the first time, enjoy the chilling and erotic tales of vampires, demon lovers, and ghostly visitations in These Haunted Dreams. A visionary artist sees too deeply into the secret life of one of his models. A businessman obsessed with time runs late for work and changes his life forever. A new homeowner discovers that his beloved residence is alive and has no intention of letting him leave. And many more...

ISBN-13: 978-0615166575 208 pages $18.95 USD

Claws of T'brisk

John X. Grey

In this horror fiction and suspense masterpiece by John X. Grey, the reader is lead along the adventures in coming of age story of our heroine Hayley Ann White. *Claws of T'brisk* tells the tale of a girl as she is pursued through the remote regions of Anchorage Alaska by hunters and werewolves alike. As her friends panic around her, can she put her trust in a young man, Peter Gorski, who appears before her in the midst of the terror.

ISBN-13: 978-1479383702

$19.99 USD

400 pages

Dark of the Night: An anthology of shadows
Dark Moon Press

Dark of the Night: An anthology of Shadows is the first anthology collection from Dark Moon, consisting of a wide variety of contributing authors from around the world. Prepare yourself for tales of outcast angels, vampire and jaunts down the macabre twists and turns of melancholy minds and more.

ISBN-13: 978-1430309154

160 pages

$16.95 USD

Dark of the Night: II An anthology of shadows
Dark Moon Press

Dark of the Night: An anthology of Shadows is the first anthology collection from Dark Moon, consisting of a wide variety of contributing authors from around the world. Prepare yourself for tales of outcast angels, vampire and jaunts down the macabre twists and turns of melancholy minds and more.

TBA pages

$19.99 USD

The Day the Circus Came to Town

Dark Moon Press

The Day the Circus Came to Town and other short stories Visions of a circus are usually fun and exciting, but to some people, with the fierce animals and rampant phobias of clowns, the excitement can easily be replaced with terror. Such is the case in the latest work, The Day the Circus Came to Town by horror writer Kevin Eads Various chilling and horrific tales of the circus such as when a freak show group takes vengeance on fanatical hecklers in The Day the Circus Came to Town, The Sad Clown, The Tale of the Amish Vampire, a artist serial killer wrecks havoc in The Art of the Kill. All brought to you from the bizarre and depraved mind of the author of The Elizabeth Bathory series, and Return to Camp Hell. Warning, these tales are not for the faint of heart or those offended by vulgarity and murderous clowns

ISBN-13: 978-1475079296 $19.99 USD

The Amulet of Elizabeth Bathory and other short stories

Kevin Eads

Vampire short stories with a classic Horror Hammer films influence. Author K. J. Eads brings you a new collection to the vampire genre that will leave you on the edge of your seat.

ISBN-13: 978-0976698425

320 pages

$19.99 USD

Lord Byron's Revenge and other short stories

Kevin Eads

Vampire short stories with a classic Horror Hammer films influence. Author Kevin Eads second book in the trilogy collection to the vampire and classic horror genre.

ISBN-13: 978-1466341555

380 pages

$19.99 USD

Dracula's Disciples and other short stories

Kevin Eads

Vampire short stories with a classic Horror Hammer films influence. Author Kevin Eads third book in the trilogy collection to the vampire and classic horror genre.

ISBN-13: 978-1467906111

$19.99 USD

324 pages

That Sure Doesn't Taste like Pork Sausage

Kevin Eads

Kevin Eads, the author of The Amulet of Elizabeth Bathory series of vampire fiction brings you his short stories of murderous politicians who stop at nothing to secure their place in power, only to be driven to madness! Murder, mayhem, and the supernatural mixed with a sense of humor Hannibal Lector would enjoy!

ISBN-13: 978-1468182071

140 pages

$17.99

Return to Camp Hell

Kevin Eads

Horror play-write and author Kevin Eads brings you his screenplays that are a tribute to classic slasher horror genre. Three tales of killers fill these pages with the writer's twisted humor added in. A fantastic read!

ISBN-13: 978-1468186666

300 pages

$19.99

Edgar Allan Poe's Lost Adventure
Kevin Eads

Horror author Kevin Eads switches gears and brings you another world in which steam punk and history collide in which Edgar Allan Poe is a vampire killer, traveling across Europe in search for his wife's murderer.

$19.95 USD

ISBN-13: 978-1477513774

296 pages

Lilith's General
Kevin Eads

Kevin Eads, the author of *The Amulet of Elizabeth Bathory* series of vampire fiction, brings you his short stories of *Lilith's General*, a vampire who has been around doing the bidding of the Queen of Darkness yet learns to be more human as time moves on. Many other short stories fill the book, such *as Club Vampires, The Love of a Vampire, The Night Watchman* and more.

ISBN-13: 978-1475257724

$17.99 USD

138 pages

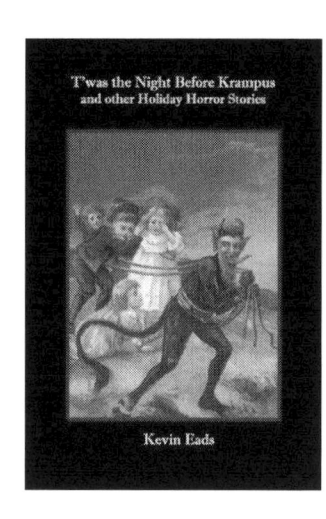

T'Was the Night Before Krampus and other Holiday Horror Stories

Kevin Eads

Macabre holidays stories, ranging from eerie to twisted from a Thanksgiving mall shooting spree, an evil Santa and many more!

172 pages
ISBN-13: 978-1478311263
$19.95 USD

The Fun House Murders

Kevin Eads

Enter a world of insanity, deception and murder as horror novelist and screen writer Kevin Eads brings you several tales of intrigue and his wicked sense of humor.

ISBN-13: 978-1477514108
252 pages
$17.99 USD

Dark Culture/Philosophy

Girls Vampire Vixens and Satan's Sirens

Corvis Nocturnum and *Old Nick Magazine*

Introduction by Gavin Baddeley

Dark Moon Press brings you this collection of beautiful women from the shadowy underground world of the Gothic subculture, living vampire community and other alternative lifestyles. The author of *Embracing the Darkness: Understanding Dark Subcultures* shares the beauty found in this seductive and hauntingly beautiful world with detailed descriptions of types, and thoughts from the women he has met. Hundreds of gorgeous photos and photographers are in full color.

WARNING: Some mild adult content

8.5x11 inches ISBN-13: 978-1479220885 $39.99

Gothic Dreamscapes

Patrick E. Flanagan

Patrick E. Flanagan is a Gothic photographer and poet whose works have been showcased in galleries and colleges in the Midwest. His breathtaking photographs will draw you into the netherworld, and his elegant prose of deep introspective poetry will leave you enthralled.

ISBN-13: 978-0976698418

178 pages

$19.99 USD

Dark *Visions: the art of Corvis Nocturnum*

From the introduction of Joseph Vargo:

"The imagery that is depicted in the art of Corvis Nocturnum is at times surreal, stark and unsettling, yet there is an underlying beauty to be found within each painting. As a writer, Corvis boldly strives to shed light on the dark subcultures of the world and his libertine attitude carries over into his artwork, which unflinchingly examines similar taboo topics. Unrestricted by conventional boundaries, his Satanic and erotic themes truly embrace the darkness within his soul. His artwork mixes traditional Gothic elements such as ravens and vampires with fallen angels and S&M vixens to create raw impressions of a dark and unadulterated realm."

WARNING: Some mild adult content Full color.

ISBN-13: 978-1478366003   8.5x11 inches 124 pages

$29.99

Courting the Poetic Craft

Drake Mefestta

Beautiful and haunting works by musician Drake Mefestta captures the powerful emotions in his stunningly detailed art. Poetry from his music and art that ranges from surreal and horrific to breathtaking to spiritually uplifting, the artist displays his inner mind's eye to the world. Gothic monoliths serve as the backdrop for angels, demons, and visions of a 'Alice in Gothic Wonderland' will enthrall you in its dreamlike quality.

8.5x11 full color 108 pages

ISBN-13: 978-1466495258 $39.99

Embracing the Darkness: Understanding Dark Subcultures

Corvis Nocturnum

Author Corvis Nocturnum brings you an unprecedented collection of Satanists, vampires, modern primitives, dark pagans, and Gothic ic artists, all speaking to you in their own words. These are people who have taken something most others find frightening or destructive, and woven it into amazing acts of creativity and spiritual vision. Corvis himself is a dark artist and visionary, and so it is with the eye of a kindred spirit that he has sought these people out to share their stories with you.

ISBN-13: 978-0976698401

242 pages

$17.95 USD

Into the Inferno: The Ninth Gate Magazine collection 1-7

Corvis Nocturnum

Dark Moon Press brings you the collected works of all six issues of *The Ninth Gate Magazine*, reformatted and includes the never seen final issue! A mixture of dark underground publications of its kind, it focused on authors, artists, bands and articles from Occult, Satanism and Vampire subculture and dark pop culture overall. Some of the people featured are Joseph Vargo, Michelle Belanger, Raven Digitalis, and Christopher Penzack, members of the Church of Satan such as Marilyn Mansfield, Magister Paradise and more. A unique collectable printing!

ISBN 9781105429323

8.5x11 in, 324 pages

$29.99 USD

My Gothic Journal
Ligeia Resurrected

Dark Moon Press is proud to offer a unique journal to pen your darkest thoughts, wistful poetry, inspired by Ligeia Resurrected. Her interior art and graphic design of stationary will be your place to record memories, a treasure trove in years to come and source for reflection.

160 pages

$9.99 USD

Goth: The Guide For Babybats and Beyond
Ligeia, Adrienne Gomez

Dark Moon Press brings you an insight to life as a young member of the Gothic subculture, as told by Ligeia Resurrected. Her topics range from how to talk to your parents about being different, bullies and the public's negative reaction to Goths, makeup and fashion tips and much more.

180 pages
$17.99 USD
FALL 2013

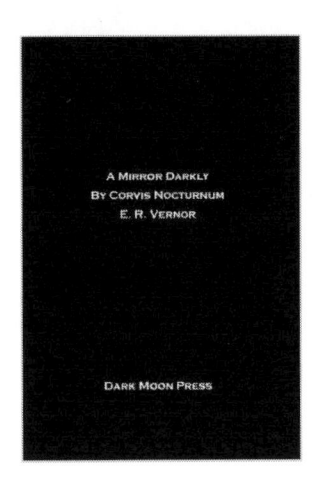

A Mirror Darkly

Corvis Nocturnum

Corvis Nocturnum, author of the well received *Embracing the Darkness; Understanding Dark Subcultures*, brings you his personal collection of essays penned from years of observing his fellow man. Few authors since Nietzsche or LaVey have so vehemently rallied against societal, religious and governmental hypocrisies, laughable shortcomings and failings. Sharply critical of apathetic bottom feeders and thoughtfully introspective, Corvis forces us to look at the creature that stares back at us from the abyss.

ISBN-13: 978-0615458168

172 pages

$16.95 USD

The Prince

Nicolo Machiavelli

When it comes to Politics, war and love, Machiavelli asserts it is a bond which men, being scoundrels, may break whenever it serves their advantage to do so; but fear is supported by the dread of pain, which is ever present. His profound understanding of the mind and heart of man, stripped of altruism is stark and honest - his statements about society and human nature that few have matched since. Now, Dark Moon Press brings you this classic rulebook that is as instrumental today as when it was first penned!

ISBN-13: 978-1460970140

124 pages

$9.95 USD

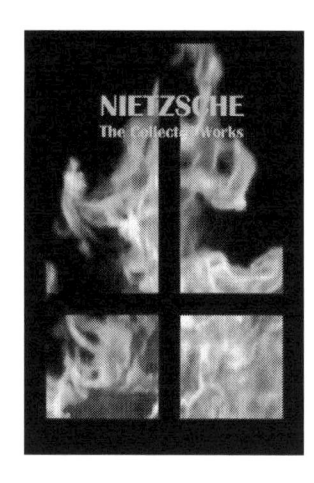

Nietzche: The Collected Works
Dark Moon Press

One of the most radical and influencial philosophers of this age is collected by Dark Moon Press. *The Anti-Christ, Beyond Good and Evil* and several works comprise this vehement intellectual of the man who coined "Will to Power! A must for any free thinker.

$29.99

300 pages

Serial Killers Murders Next Door
Bud Weiser

The serial killer next door doesn't always get mass news coverage for decades like Jack the Ripper, Ted Bundy or Ed Gein. Often, killers who prey on massive amount of victims never even make much of a ripple in history. *Serial Killers Murders Next Door*
Bud Weiser

$19.99

Fall 2013

ORDER FORM

P.O. Box 11496

Fort Wayne, Indiana 46858-1496

www.DarkMoonPress.com

DarkMoon@DarkMoonPress.com

Quantity	Title	Price	Total Price
	THANK YOU FOR YOUR ORDER!!		

Please make all checks/money orders payable to: Dark Moon Press. All nonsufficient funds will be charged the cost of all fees by the bank plus $25.

*Shipping in the continental United States is $3.00 for the first book, and $2.00 per additional title. Please contact us for international postal rates, thank you!

Please allow for postal and federal holidays which will delay shipping. Wholesale accounts are available for special pricing, see vendor application.

*Shipping:

Total:

Printed in Great Britain
by Amazon